Last Days Heroes:

Becoming a Hero of Faith for the End Times

Second Edition

By
Dwight E.Link

In memory of Wesley Blumer - mentor, teacher, and faithful guide. You showed me that true strength is found in humility, and that the quietest voices often carry the deepest wisdom.

You kept me scripturally grounded and spiritually anchored, and I am forever grateful.

You are deeply missed, until we meet again.

Table of Contents

Introduction 1

Chapter 1: A Couple of My Heroes 7

Chapter 2: The Hero Who Couldn't Be Found 20

Chapter 3: Heroes of Faith 26

Chapter 4: Believing in What You Can't See 36

Chapter 5: The Fight for a Soul 45

Chapter 6: When God Speaks 60

Chapter 7: The Link to Hope 76

Chapter 8: The Fall 94

Chapter 9: The End-Time War 109

Chapter 10: Get Ready 125

Epilogue 131

Last Days Heroes Bible Study Guide 133

Introduction

What Are the "Last Days"? A Closer Look

When people hear the phrase *last days*, it often stirs up images of the end of the world, catastrophic events, or even sensational headlines. But biblically, the "last days" refer to a period that began with Christ's resurrection and continues until His return—a time when God's ultimate plan for humanity is moving toward fulfillment. Unlike popular interpretations that only focus on disaster, the biblical meaning is about the culmination of God's promises and the call for people to turn their hearts toward Him. Think of it less as a countdown to destruction and more as a season of urgency and preparation.

To clarify, when I reflect on the "last days," I picture someone who knows their time is short—like a person given a terminal diagnosis. There's a sense of urgency; every moment feels more significant. Just as warning signs for illness intensify, Scripture says we'll see signs that time is running out. How we respond to these signs makes all the difference.

Some people, faced with limited time, choose to draw close to loved ones or seek to make peace with God. Others might try to leave their mark in other ways. But one thing is certain: knowing our time short changes the way we live. The same is true spiritually. The Bible describes the last days as a time when our priorities should shift, drawing us closer to God and to one another.

The Bible gives us a description of what God calls the last days for this earth, and according to the signs we are seeing now, many believe that those days are approaching fast. After growing up in church, I've heard for years that the last days are at hand and many have questioned this. Some have even abandoned their faith because they haven't seen it yet, which in itself is a sign of the last days.

According to scripture (2 Timothy 3:1–5 NIV; Matthew 24 NIV), and I'm paraphrasing here, what we can expect as the last days approach is that people will become lovers of themselves. Right will be determined to be wrong and what is wrong and evil will be celebrated as good and right. False teachings will flood the church, and wars will increase as earthquakes are felt more frequently and in more places. Men and women will prop themselves up on high pedestals at the cost of the poor and naïve, and some will even declare themselves to be a type of messiah, if not the one and only. If you're not aware of the signs, I suggest you research them. I could give you the scripture word for word, but I'm not going to rob you of the thrill of seeking it and learning it on your own. Be a student and follower of the word, not a follower of me or any other author, teacher, or preacher. I'm simply bringing to your attention what God has placed on my heart to share, but it's up to you to discover the truth on your own through the assistance of the Holy Spirit. Trust me: there's no greater teacher than him.

The Bible calls these signs "birth pains." That term might sound strange at first, but birth pains are contractions—intense signals that new life is about to begin. At the start, there's excitement and anticipation, but as labor progresses, the pain and urgency increase. In the same way, the last days are filled with signs that things are coming to a climax, but they ultimately point to a joyful new beginning for those who trust in Christ.

This is how I see the era we're living in: the signs are increasing, and sometimes the pain is real, but hope is ahead. Even in times of suffering or confusion, we can look forward to what God has promised.

An important thing to remember is that God is very patient and is holding off the final days in hopes that some will be saved (2 Peter 3:9 NIV). It's in the Bible. Look it up. But as we wait and watch as evil abounds, while the murder of innocent babies is worshiped, sexual immorality in all forms is celebrated, and thieves and liars are hailed as great leaders, what type of person are we to be? Second Peter 3 (NIV) is a great place to start when trying to answer this question. It gives us many guidelines and commandments about who we are to be as we wait for his second coming.

If you haven't already, I highly suggest that you make it a regular part of your study. God's word is very clear in the fact that if we don't follow his word, then we will not enter his kingdom (Matthew 7:21 NIV). Not only does your eternity depend on your understanding of the truth, but so do others who depend on you sharing that knowledge & freedom that you've come to know.

So, who are we called to be? In these last days, I believe God calls us to be something more than just spectators or casual believers. In a word: **heroes**.

More specifically, a **hero of faith**—someone who trusts God deeply, stands strong when others falter, and lives out their faith in real, courageous ways. Unlike the world's definition of a hero (someone admired for bravery or achievement), a hero of faith is marked by trust in God, sacrificial love, and a willingness to be used by Him, even when it's difficult.

This might not look like the kind of hero the world celebrates, but it's the kind God honors.

A hero of faith is the person who steps forward when no one else will, who brings hope to the hopeless, and who refuses to settle for a watered-down faith. I remember a time when I faced a deeply hopeless season—when faith felt powerless and routine. It was during that time that a friend reached out and prayed with me, challenging me to seek God honestly and wholeheartedly. That moment changed the direction of my life and showed me what it means to be a hero of faith for someone else.

What Is a Hero?

Generally, we define a hero as someone admired for courage or noble character. But who decides what's truly heroic? For some, a hero is an athlete or celebrity; for others, a parent who persevered through hardship. The point is, the world's definition changes, but a hero of faith is measured by their trust and obedience to God.

If you ask a child who their hero is, you'll get some pretty entertaining answers. When I was a kid, my hero was the creepy dude who drove the ice cream truck around the neighborhood and always seemed to arrive at just the right time—when I was broke.

But as we grow older, our idea of what makes up a hero changes. As teenagers, many look to professional athletes as heroes, or we may even idolize a movie star or musician. As adults, our heroes change even more.

I look at the men of WWII who stormed the beaches of Normandy and parachuted in on D-Day as true heroes. We may look up to historical figures, parents, or biblical leaders like Joshua—a man who needed to be reminded repeatedly to be strong and courageous. That encouragement resonates with me. I even have Joshua 1:9 tattooed on my forearm as a daily reminder to lean on God's strength, not my own.

But here's the transition: This book isn't about famous heroes or even the ones you might name. It's about the hero who could have been but wasn't—and the hero who must rise in these days. Not a hero who brings revolution, but one who sparks revival. Not one who tears down, but one who helps restore and save. A hero of faith.

Who is your hero? Take a moment to think about that question. Maybe you have several, but who stands out most clearly in your mind? It's not about a group or a title—it's about a person whose life made a difference in yours.

I encourage you to reflect on who that person is—maybe a family member, a biblical figure, or someone you know personally. And then, ask yourself: what made them a hero to you?

So, who did you name as your hero? Was it a family member? An athlete? Maybe your hero is a member of the military or wears a badge every day. Maybe you chose one of the many biblical characters who went above and beyond their abilities to achieve God's will. Certainly Moses, David, Sampson, and so many others qualify as heroes.

For me, it's the biblical warrior Joshua. He is the soldier's soldier. A military genius who overcame surmountable odds, one of those being his fear to lead a nation to the Promised Land. Being a former soldier myself, there's one way that I can relate to Joshua. I too must be reminded constantly to be strong and courageous and to rely on God's ability instead of my own. I even have "Joshua 1:9 NIV" tattooed on my forearm, along with my jump wings, as a daily reminder to be strong and courageous. But it also serves as a reminder of a time when I was strong and courageous.

But this book is not about Joshua or the many heroes you may have listed. This book is about a hero who could have been but never was. It's about a hero who never was but can be. It's about a hero who must confront unprecedented threats to humanity during these turbulent end-times—a hero whose rise is critical, for without them, hope may fade and darkness could prevail. The stakes are higher than ever, and this hero's courage and faith will determine whether revival and restoration can overcome the chaos threatening our world. It's not about a hero who will bring revolution but revival. Not a hero who will slay many but save many. A true hero of faith. Will that hero exist in you or in me?

As you read, you'll notice I often encourage you to "look it up" for yourself. Don't just take my word for it—explore the Scriptures. The journey to faith is deeply personal, and there's no substitute for firsthand discovery. One sermon or one book isn't enough; we need to pursue truth daily.

I'll be honest: I'm not the most likely candidate to write a book like this. School was a struggle, and I know what it's like to feel unqualified. But I'm encouraged by the fact that God often chooses the unlikely and the ordinary—just like the disciples, who amazed everyone by their boldness despite some being uneducated. God can use anyone who is willing. That's what I long to see in myself and in each of us: a willingness to be available to God in these last days.

The stories and lessons ahead aren't always easy, but they're real. I want to show you that God's power can restore, redeem, and use anyone. If you're feeling hopeless or unworthy, I hope my journey gives you hope. I've witnessed firsthand the mercy and transformation God offers.The road might not always be easy, but it's worth every step.

My prayer is that this book will encourage you, challenge you, and remind you that you are never beyond God's reach. Let's begin this journey together, seeking truth, growing in faith, and becoming the heroes this world needs.

May these pages inspire, challenge, and bless you as you discover what it means to be a hero of faith in the last days.

Now, let's begin the search for that last day's hero of faith starting with you and me.

Chapter 1: A Couple of My Heroes

In today's world, technology and social media put a spotlight on heroes like never before. My social feeds are full of memes and posts honoring our military, police officers, firefighters, EMTs, and others who serve and protect our communities. I'm grateful for this public recognition—these brave men and women absolutely deserve it. Our Vietnam veterans are finally receiving some of the long-overdue honor they deserve, and I hope one day security officers will be celebrated in the same way, rather than just being remembered as punchlines in mall comedies. Thank you, Paul Blart, for at least starting that conversation.

These men and women have made the conscious decision to put themselves on the line—defending, protecting, and sometimes even saving lives. Many have sacrificed everything. They are worthy of our deepest gratitude and respect. Scripture reminds us that "greater love has no one than this: to lay down one's life for another." I have witnessed that kind of selflessness, and I know I can never thank them enough.

While these individuals are rightly celebrated, I've also been shaped by heroes much closer to home— people whose quiet courage may never make headlines but has deeply influenced my life. For me, heroism is not just found on the battlefield or in acts of public service; sometimes, it's found in everyday moments and the steadfastness of ordinary people.

Don't get me wrong, nothing I share here is meant to minimize the sacrifice of those who wear a uniform. Their heroism is in a category all its own. But each of us, if we look back, can probably name personal heroes—individuals whose courage, sacrifice, or quiet character left a permanent mark on our lives. The heroes I want to tell you about in this chapter are personal, and their stories may never make the evening news. Before we search for a hero who could not be found, let me introduce you to one of mine.

As a former soldier, I never considered myself a hero, and most soldiers I know would say the same.

We didn't sign up for medals or restaurant discounts, most of us simply believed that freedom was worth more than our own comfort. For some, military service was the only path they saw forward, while others felt a calling to serve. Whatever brought us there, the willingness to risk our lives for something greater mattered.

Too often, we take for granted those who make our freedoms possible, sometimes even using those freedoms to criticize the very system that protects us. That can be frustrating, but it's also part of what

freedom means. It's more than just speaking your mind or carrying a weapon; it's costly, paid for by people willing to stand in harm's way. I salute them all. And though I may not call myself a hero, I'm grateful to have known and served with at least one. As you read on, I invite you to think about the quiet heroes in your own life, the ones whose influence might never go viral, but whose impact is lasting and real.

PFC Vance "Troy" Coats

Did you ever make a choice and then, on the day it was time to act, instantly wish you hadn't? Honestly, I was at the point where I wanted to yell, "Sweet mercy, what have I done?" That pretty much summed up day one of boot camp.

It was February 1989 when I arrived at Ft. Benning Georgia. At reception, we were issued two duffel bags full of gear, then loaded up on a cattle car and hauled off to what would become our home for the next several weeks. We arrived at our unit full of anticipation. We stepped off the trailers in front of our barracks, slung our duffel bags over our shoulders, and started walking toward the building. I remember thinking, *this might not be so bad after all.*

Then I saw him.

The dreaded drill sergeant we had all been warned about was coming straight toward me like I had insulted his mother or something. That was hard for me to process, because I'm a very likable guy. He was joined by a few other monsters just as big and angry as he was, and before long they had us holding our duffel bags out to our sides while they screamed at us and called us every name imaginable, and some you can't even imagine. If that was not bad enough, we then had to run laps around the buildings carrying those duffle bags at our sides. After a few exhausting laps, we were ordered to dump everything out onto the ground while the drill sergeants kicked our belongings in all different directions, mixing it up with surrounding soldiers.

One of drill instructors decided to do what I now know was a toothpaste check. In case you are unfamiliar with that term, it means a mentally disturbed person grabs your tube of toothpaste, removes the cap, and squeezes the entire thing all over your clothes. If this ever happens to you, let me offer some advice: do not tell the disturbed individual that he owes you fifty cents for wasting your toothpaste. That will not improve the situation. It will only lead to more yelling and more push-ups.

Later we learned that this lovely welcome was called shock treatment. It worked beautifully. I was both shocked and treated. But looking back now, I can say it was one of the most important days of my life. I wouldn't change it for anything. Well, I might have hidden my toothpaste better. And I would have learned to keep my mouth shut sooner. When sarcasm is one of your gifts, it is hard not to share it with the world. I found out that basic training is not the place to share that gift.

One day we were standing in line—one of the thousands of lines I would stand in during training—and I made a comment to the guy behind me. I was just trying to lighten the mood. Apparently, I spoke louder than I realized, because the entire line burst out laughing.

Everyone laughed except one person. You guessed it: the drill instructor.

I do not remember what I said. It was probably something Bill Murray would have said in *Stripes*. But I do remember what happened next. I found myself in the front-leaning rest position to start knocking out some push-ups. But not ordinary push-ups. Each one was to be counted off with "one I'm a sh*t bird, two I'm a sh*t bird……………" you get the idea.

This created a problem for me. I was a Christian and I didn't use foul language.

So, to my own surprise, I said, "I can't do that, Drill Sergeant."

He gave me a look both shocked and puzzled. He shouted back, clearly not accustomed to being told no, "And why not, Private?"

I answered, "Because I'm a Christian, and I won't say that."

I braced for impact, unsure of what would happen next. However, to my astonishment, he revised the phrase to a more appropriate alternative that was acceptable to both parties. I did my fifty doodie bird push-ups while the rest of the platoon enjoyed the show. But I noticed something after that. That drill instructor respected me for standing up for my faith, and so did many of the others in that line.

That is one reason you stand for your faith no matter the cost. In the end, you may win more respect than ridicule. I only wish I could say I stayed faithful to God throughout my years in the service. Sadly, I cannot. More about that later.

That day taught me two things: standing for your convictions matters, and so does knowing when to keep your mouth shut. As for that drill instructor, he eventually became my favorite. I learned a lot from him.

Days passed, and soon I found myself forming bonds with others in my platoon. After the initial shock wore off, a deep camaraderie began to grow among us. We were all thrown together, stripped of old identities, and forced to rely on one another in ways none of us expected. That's when I met Troy Coats.

Troy and I both enlisted as grunts and began our training at the Infantry School in Georgia. We were fortunate enough to be assigned to the same platoon, and we hit it off from the beginning. Everyone hit it off with Troy though. You couldn't help but like they guy. He had the classic all-American-boy look and attitude to match.

We had both signed up for airborne school, excited by the idea of becoming paratroopers. I still remember our first jump together, which was also when I discovered my fear of heights. The green light came on, signaling it was time to exit. Troy launched himself out of the aircraft, but apparently not hard enough— because he hit the plane with his face on the way out. Not exactly how you want your first jump to go. But later, on the ground, with his face bruised and swollen, Troy just grinned and said, "It was awesome!" That was Troy—he could take a rough landing and turn it into a story that made everyone laugh.

On another jump, I was farther back in the stick, all hooked up and waiting for the green light to go. When it came on, the stick started to move but then suddenly stopped. Then I heard a bloodcurdling scream: "Nooooooo!"

I looked toward the door and saw a young woman clinging to both sides of the opening like a cat being lowered into a bathtub. She was refusing to jump. The jumpmaster calmly convinced her to let go by telling her they would unhook her and sit her down.

She let go.

They threw her out.

They meant it when they said that if you got on that bird, there was only one way you were getting off.

To her credit, she ended up doing fine and found out that she loved it. My second jump, however, did not go nearly as well.

As I came down, I was drifting backward. The jumpmasters on the ground were yelling instructions through megaphones, trying to help me prepare for a backward parachute landing fall. I hated the backward landing. I never could get the hang of it. So instead of listening, I started bicycle-pedaling in the air, trying to turn myself to land on my side. I did not make it. I landed on my heels, then my head, and then everything went dark.

When I came to, a jumpmaster was standing over me with his megaphone in my face, screaming obscenities and doing his best to convince me that I was, in fact, a moron. He continued shouting while I gathered my chute and staggered off the drop zone. If you ever played that game where you spin around a baseball bat and then try to run in a straight line, that is more or less what I looked like.

Thankfully, the rest of my jumps went fine. Earning my jump wings was one of the proudest moments of my life. But before we were able to get to Airborne School and them, we still had to finish infantry school.

When we enlisted, Coats and I were both classified as 11X-Ray, which meant we had no assigned duty station yet. The Army could send us anywhere in the world. Throughout most of our sixteen weeks of training, we had no idea where we would end up. We were told that many new infantrymen wound up in Korea, and I did not want to spend my first year in the Army separated from my wife on the DMZ.

As our training wrapped up and airborne school approached, our drill instructors called us into formation and handed out our assignments. Thankfully, God had heard my prayers. Because we were heading to airborne school, we were assigned to the 82nd Airborne Division. We were thrilled. We were going to be paratroopers in one of the most elite units in the Army. We sat around the barracks imagining what life in the 82nd would be like.

That excitement did not last long.

Around that time, President Noriega was in the news over Panama. I did not know much about the country. I only knew it was jungle and far from home. Then one day at formation, one of our drill sergeants made an announcement I will never forget:

"If you are assigned to the 82nd, you are now on alert for possible deployment to Panama."

Suddenly Korea did not sound so bad.

That night the mood in the barracks changed. The excitement was gone. It is a strange thing: you join the Army to fight for your country, you train for it, and you tell yourself you are ready for it. But when the possibility becomes real, it still knots up your insides. At least it did mine. And that night, I had a conversation with Troy that I have never forgotten. Even after all these years, I can still hear it.

A few of us had grown close by then, and we would gather in a corner of the barracks and talk about home, the Army, and whatever was weighing on us. That night we were talking about Panama, trying to imagine what it would be like. I did my best to put on a brave face and talk like a young soldier ready to jump in and handle business. But inside, I was scared.

Then I noticed the look on Troy's face.

He did not just look nervous. He looked burdened. We asked him what was wrong, and with tears in his eyes he said, "I'm going to die in Panama."

I did not know what to say. I gave him the standard answer you give in moments like that. I told him he was just nervous, that we all were, and that everything was going to be okay.

But he looked at us again, with tears flowing and said, "You don't understand. I'm going to die in Panama."

We did our best to comfort him. We told him he was a good soldier. We told him God would watch over him. Eventually the conversation moved on. We finished training, earned our jump wings, and then went to Ft. Bragg for our duty assignments.

That was the last time I ever spoke to Troy.

He deployed to Panama and gave his life during Operation Just Cause. I found out while watching the news, when the names of those killed in action were shown on the screen. He was one of them.

PFC Vance Troy Coats was a hero. Troy's courage and friendship continue to inspire me. I often think about his laughter echoing through the barracks, the way he looked out for others without any expectation of praise, and how, even in the face of fear, his heart remained open and honest. His memory reminds all of the cost of service and the importance of cherishing those we meet along the way.

Troy taught me that heroism isn't just about the battles we face, but about the spirit and kindness we bring to those around us—especially when the world feels uncertain. I will never forget him, and I hope his story reminds us all to honor the quiet, steadfast heroes who walk beside us, often unseen but never unappreciated.

Small Hero, Big Results

The definition of a hero also includes someone admired for courage. Sometimes you do not have to look far to find that kind of person. For many of us, that hero is found in our own family.

There are many things in life that require courage to endure. Cancer is one of them. Most of us know someone who has faced it, and maybe you have faced it yourself. For me, one of the clearest examples of courage I have ever seen was in my daughter Ashley. She did not just face cancer once. She beat it twice. And let me tell you, she handled it a whole lot better than I did.

I once heard a song by Scott Stapp called "Purpose for the Pain." I did not understand that phrase when my daughter was diagnosed with osteosarcoma at ten years old. What possible purpose could there be in a child enduring that kind of pain? You hear about those things happening to other families, but you never think it is going to happen to yours—especially when you have prayed over your children and placed them in the hands of God.

It did not make sense to me, and I responded the way many people do when they are operating in the flesh: I got angry. Very angry. I wrestled with every emotion I could think of. I wondered what I had done wrong, what sin I had committed, and why God would allow my daughter to suffer like that. Eventually I stopped asking questions and started blaming Him. I reached the point where I thought, *if this is how God is going to treat us, then why bother praying at all?*

That was the problem. Christianity lived in the flesh never works. I turned away from God in my heart, and I am thankful beyond words that He is patient and merciful.

No parent should have to watch their child suffer through cancer, and no child should have to endure it. But what I saw in my little girl amazed me. Through the chemo, the surgeries, the pain, and the sickness, she never lost her smile. More importantly, she never lost her faith. Even when the treatments made her miserable, she was still joking with the nurses. We heard repeatedly how she brightened people's days. She quickly became a favorite at the hospital.

My wife and I had always tried to raise our children to trust God no matter what. Yet there I was, losing my own grip. I would put on a brave face for Ashley and say a prayer so she would feel encouraged, but inside I felt empty. I was ashamed of that. My wife, on the other hand, was steady through it all. She may tell you otherwise, but I know better. She was a rock.

We had two other children at home, so while my wife stayed with Ashley at the hospital, I stayed back with the others and kept working my full-time job. Gehrig and Brienna were wonderful throughout that season. They encouraged their sister and helped more than children should ever have to. Friends, family, and our small-town community in Oklahoma also stepped up in an incredible way. People brought help, encouragement, and support when we needed it most. We will never forget that.

As for my faith, I did not know where it was anymore. I lived in anger and confusion, and I thought I was hiding it well. Maybe I fooled other people, but I was not fooling God.

One of the burdens that comes with serious illness is financial weight. The journey back and forth to Oklahoma City was expensive, but I refused to pray about it. My thinking was simple: if God had prevented this, we would not be in this situation to begin with. So instead of praying, I sat in my chair, studied the budget, and tried to figure out what we needed for gas, bills, and hospital trips. I would think about it constantly, but I would not pray.

And yet, before the next week came, there would be a knock at the door. A neighbor. A friend. Someone from town.

They would hand me money and say the same thing in one form or another: "I felt like God wanted me to bring this to you. I hope it helps."

And it always did.

Sometimes it happened at the grocery store. Sometimes on Main Street. Sometimes at the front door. The amount was often close to what I had calculated we needed, and sometimes even more. Then came the hospital bill for around $98,000. I do not know about you, but I did not have ninety-eight thousand dollars sitting around. A few weeks later, we were notified that the bill had been paid in full by the nuns at Mercy, and we owed nothing.

That got my attention.

I kept being reminded of the truth that God is faithful even when we are not. I still would not pray for it. I would only think about what we needed, and somehow the provision would come. Little by little, God was wearing down my resistance.

Then one day I was in my home gym working out when I felt a strong urge to pick up my Bible and open it. I resisted at first, but eventually I gave in. I opened it and read, "If you return to the Almighty, you will be restored." In Job's situation, those words were not a correct assessment of his condition. But for me, they broke me wide open. I wept uncontrollably. Right there in my weight room, God restored my faith and gave me a peace and comfort that I cannot fully describe.

It was a long year, and there were more surgeries still to come. But because my little girl never lost her faith or her smile, her daddy found his faith again. Through Ashley's suffering, I came to know God in a deeper way. For that reason, she is one of my heroes.

As my prayer life returned and my faith grew stronger, I began hearing the phrase "Link to Hope." I did not know what it meant, but I knew it mattered. Over time, I let it drift into the background and went on with life. Then, five years later, Ashley's cancer returned, this time in her lung. But by then, I was not the same man. Instead of getting angry at God, I asked Him, "What are You trying to tell me now?" And once again, I began hearing: "Link to Hope."

The doctors removed cancer from her lung, and she endured another year of chemotherapy. Once again, God brought her through it. We both came out of that season stronger. I still did not fully understand what "Link to Hope" meant, but in time God revealed it.

So, do Troy and Ashley qualify as heroes? Maybe not by everyone's definition. But to me, they absolutely do. Each faced a battle they did not choose, and each thought of others in the middle of it. Troy went into Panama knowing he might not come home, but he went because duty called. Ashley, even in pain, kept smiling and bringing hope to others around her. Even as a child, she seemed to understand that God had a purpose, no matter the outcome.

God does not create people without purpose. Every person He brings into this world has gifts, abilities, and opportunities meant to glorify Him. The real question is whether we will use those things for His purposes or for our own selfish ambitions. As much as I love America, I believe many Christians have been harmed by chasing the so-called American dream more than the will of God. Our goal should not be to build paradise for ourselves on earth. Our goal should be to use what God has given us to serve and bless others. Scripture is clear about that.

You may not realize it, but when you feed someone who is hungry, give a coat to someone who is cold, or visit an elderly person in a nursing home who has no one, you become a hero in that person's eyes. Sometimes the smallest acts of kindness make the biggest impact. And when we do those things for the least of these, we do them for God.

That is the kind of hero He is looking for in the last days.

Selfless. Truth-seeking. Full of love. Willing to stand for Him no matter what the cost. Will you be one?

Chapter 2:
The Hero Who Couldn't Be Found

What if heroes did not exist?

What if no one had been willing to storm the beaches of Normandy? What if no one had taken the oath to protect and serve, or to defend the Constitution? What if Joshua had told God, "Thanks, but no thanks"?

What if David had decided Goliath was simply too big and the risk was not worth it?

Can you imagine what America would be like if our Founding Fathers had decided that the fight for freedom was not worth the cost? Not just America, but much of the world would be different. Tyranny would reign, and many of the freedoms we take for granted would not exist.

I do believe that the word *hero* is too small to describe Jesus Christ. But what about His disciples? What if they had gone back to their old lives and ignored His command to wait for the promise of the Holy Spirit? Would the church even exist as we know it today? It is not hard to see that without heroes—without men and women willing to stand against evil and obey God—the world would be a far darker and more hopeless place.

We have already talked about what people consider a hero, and I have shared a couple of my own. But who would God call a hero? Does He view people that way at all?

God does not idolize people the way we do. He does not worship His creation; we were created to worship Him. Yet Scripture makes it clear that He does notice faithfulness, obedience, righteousness, and truth. So, the question is not whether God is impressed by celebrity, talent, status, or power. The question is whether He is looking for a certain kind of person.

To answer that, we need to begin with the hero who could not be found.

So, who was this missing hero? This man who had the potential to bring deliverance to an entire nation, yet did not exist when he was needed?

We find him or rather, fail to find him—in the book of Jeremiah.

Once again, God's people had turned away from Him. They had forgotten what He had delivered them from. They had embraced false gods, believed lies, and rejected the way of their Redeemer in order to walk down the path of destruction. Because of that rebellion, judgment was coming. But what stood out to me most in Jeremiah 5 was not just the sin of the people. It was the heart of God in the middle of it.

God told the prophet to search Jerusalem thoroughly—to go up and down the streets, through the squares, from place to place. In other words, search everywhere. But what was he looking for?

One man.

One person who dealt honestly and sought the truth.

That is remarkable. Out of an entire city headed toward judgment, God said that if even one righteous person could be found, He would forgive the whole city. He was not looking for a military hero, a politician, a celebrity, or some larger-than-life champion. He was looking for a person marked by truth and righteousness. He was looking for a hero of faith.

And that person could not be found.

That is what makes this chapter so sobering. It was not merely that Jerusalem was sinful. It was that no one could be found who loved truth enough, loved God enough, and walked uprightly enough to stand in the gap. The one person who might have changed the course of the city's history was nowhere to be found. And when that finally hit me, I began to understand the power one righteous person can carry in the hands of God.

For years, when I read passages like this, my attitude was often, *well, Jerusalem had it coming.* I would think, *Look out. Judgment is on the way.* The cycle seemed obvious. God delivered His people, they followed Him for a while, then drifted, complained, turned to idols, suffered the consequences, cried out for help, were forgiven, and then repeated the same pattern all over again.

To be honest, I would read it and think, *how can they be so blind? How can they keep doing this after all God has done for them?*

Then one day, my own life came to mind.

And I realized I had lived through that same cycle myself more than once. That changed how I read Jeremiah 5.

Instead of simply seeing a rebellious people getting what they deserved, I saw a God who was looking for a reason to show mercy. He was searching for one faithful person. One honest seeker of truth. One life fully surrendered to Him. That was the part that gripped me. Not just the judgment, but the missing hero.

It made me start asking a different question: what can one righteous person actually do?

The answer, according to Scripture, is quite a lot. Again and again, God has accomplished His purposes through one faithful person. He used one man, Noah, to preserve a future. He used one man, Moses, to confront Pharaoh. He used one shepherd boy, David, to bring down a giant. He used one prophet, Jeremiah, to speak truth to a nation that did not want to hear it. And above all, He brought redemption to the world through one man—Jesus Christ, the Son of the living God.

That is why righteousness and obedience matter so much. Those are the things God is looking for.

Those are the things that make someone a hero in His eyes. Not fame. Not charisma. Not influence.

Truth. Faith. Obedience. Courage.

At one point, this chapter forced me to confront something in my own heart.

There have been times when I have looked at the wickedness around us—whether in Washington, in culture, or in states and cities that seem determined to celebrate what God condemns—and I have caught myself thinking, *Why does God not just judge it now?* If I am being honest, there were times when my attitude was closer to Jonah than to Jesus.

That is where the story of Jonah becomes so important.

Nineveh was a wicked city. Its evil had risen before God, and judgment was coming unless the people repented. Nineveh needed a hero of faith, someone willing to carry a message of mercy into a place he hated. Jonah was chosen for that assignment.

But Jonah did not want to go.

He did not want Nineveh to be saved. He wanted it judged. He knew that if the people repented, God would forgive them, and that was exactly what Jonah did not want. So instead of obeying, he ran the other way. He had the message that could save lives, but he did not want to deliver it.

Eventually, of course, God got Jonah where he needed to be. Jonah preached, Nineveh repented, and God showed mercy. What should have been wonderful news left Jonah angry. He still wanted judgment more than redemption. And that forced me to ask a hard question of myself:

Am I more like Jonah, or more like Jesus? That question still stings.

Because Jesus did not come for the righteous alone. He came for sinners. He did not give His life only for the people we agree with, understand, or find easy to love. He gave His life for the world. That includes the rebellious, the deceived, the immoral, the proud, the hateful, the self-righteous, and the broken. It includes people we may be tempted to write off.

So instead of praying for the destruction of the unrighteous, maybe we ought to pray for the righteous person who is still in that city. Maybe we ought to pray for the one who is dealing honestly, seeking truth, and carrying the message of salvation. Maybe we ought to pray that there will be more of them.

Those are the true heroes of faith.

A hero saves lives through action. And when a believer carries the message of Christ to someone who receives it and turns to God, more than a life has been helped. A soul has been rescued for eternity. That is a greater work than anything the world usually celebrates as heroic.

As Christians, we must understand that we are not ordinary. We carry a soul-saving message. We are called to live it and speak it with courage, no matter what it costs us. If our faith is real, then we cannot live as though we belong entirely to this world. We are called to stand apart from it while still reaching into it with truth and mercy.

So let me ask you:

If you knew that God was about to judge a city many people had already written off as hopeless, would you bargain for mercy the way Abraham did for Sodom? Or would you run in the other direction like Jonah?

Would you be willing to stand in the gap?

Would you be the one righteous person God could count on to deal honestly, seek truth, and carry His message to the lost?

Because that is the kind of hero He is looking for.

And being that kind of hero is not easy. If it were, everyone would be one.

Chapter 3: Heroes of Faith

If a real hero came upon someone drowning, he would not stop to ask whether that person was liberal or conservative, Christian or atheist, gay or straight, pro-life or pro-choice. A true hero would act. He would use whatever strength, skill, or resource he had to try to save the person in front of him.

That picture matters because, as Christians, we carry a lifesaving message. We are called to share it and live it before others regardless of what they believe, how they may respond, or what fears we may have. The way we respond to people reveals who we truly are. We may be able to hide things from others for a while, but we will never hide them from God.

If you continue reading Jeremiah 5, you will notice something sobering. God had no trouble finding people who claimed to believe in Him. The problem was deeper than that. There is a difference between believing in God and truly seeking Him. His eyes were searching for truth, and what He found instead was pretense. In other words, there were plenty of professing people, but not enough genuine ones.

We would be foolish to think that problem belongs only to ancient Jerusalem. We have our share of it today. The church has compromised with the world so often that in some places it is becoming harder to tell the difference between the two. That is why every believer must develop a real relationship with God and know His Word personally.

That is also why I keep telling you, "Look it up."

I do not want you to take my word for these things. Read Scripture for yourself. Search it. Study it. Sit with it. If you are truly seeking truth, God will reveal far more to you through His Word than I ever could. He will make things personal. He will show you what you need the very moment you need it.

The Bible tells us that there are times that we don't know what to pray and the Holy Spirit will pray on our behalf essentially pray for us. (Look it up in Romans 8:26–27 NIV). Jesus told his disciples that he would be going back to the Father and it was for their benefit. Our benefit as well because he would be sending the Holy Spirit to earth to teach us and empower us. Because of the Holy Spirit, we would even do greater things than Jesus did because he left. (Look it up in John 14:15–26 NIV).

I was sitting at home one afternoon and something was wrong. I felt heaviness within me. It was like I had done something I shouldn't have, but I had no idea what it was. The only thing I knew was that I just didn't feel right. I was watching TV and just happened to turn to a preacher I would listen to from time to time. I loved his teaching on prophecy and Israel and would watch when I had a chance. This time he was talking about how the Holy Spirit prays for us when we don't know what we ought to pray. I felt like I needed to go to my room and just begin to pray. I knelt down beside my bed. My prayer started out with "God, I'm not sure what I've done to offend you or make you mad, but I just don't feel right. Please allow your Spirit to search me and rid me of this sin or whatever it is that I've done." Shortly after that, I felt a presence enter my room and what felt like a hand placed on my back. It was such a sweet presence. I began praying in another language. I have no idea what language it was or what was being said, but it was intense. There was a conversation going on between God and the spirit within in me, and after a few minutes, there was a huge weight that was lifted and I felt free from whatever was hindering me. These are the kind of things that God loves to reveal to us when we truly seek him and search his scriptures.

So what's the key to becoming the kind of hero God is looking for today? It's in that first verse of Jeremiah 5. One who does justice and seeks truth. What's truth? Just because a person may believe something doesn't make it truth. There's man's version of truth, which is also known as lies, and then there's God's version of truth. It's getting so much more difficult to know truth from lies.

Social media has become the main stage for manipulating people. I see politicians spouting off all kinds of nonsense, and people will eat it up. I even see pastors manipulating scripture to make a point that will eventually lead people astray. Jesus made this very clear that false teachers, even back then, would teach a false religion and deceive many, even the elect (Matthew 24:24 NIV). The only truth that brings real freedom is God's truth, and his truth is found in his word. If you don't know the truth, you're not going to know when you're being lied to.

Find a good church. Listen to the pastor, and take notes. Throughout the week, study it, search it for yourself, and see if it measures up. If it does, then take it to heart, apply it to your own life, and live it out.

Seek truth! Here's something important I learned when I began seeking truth and traded in my replica Christian lifestyle for the real thing. Jesus said, "Not everyone who says to me, Lord, Lord, will enter the kingdom of heaven, but only the one who does the will of my Father who is in heaven" (Matthew 7:21 NIV). I've read this numerous times, and every time I breathe a sigh of relief because I've said the sinner's prayer and believe that Jesus is the son of God. That's all it took, right? I'm heaven bound.

One day when I was reading this verse, I felt an unsettling. Remember the Holy Spirit was sent to teach us right, so we must be teachable. That means when you're reading scripture and you get this feeling that there's more to it, then you need to stop and listen. I began to look at that part of the verse that says, "Only he who does the will of the Father." Then this interesting question popped into my head. Do I know what God's will is? I thought so. His will is to believe in him and say the sinner's prayer, right? I decided to do what God has always intended for us to do and seek the truth.

It wasn't long before I came across a statement that Paul made. "It's God's will that you be sanctified" (1 Thessalonians 4:3). It was a little alarming because I wasn't sure what *sanctified* meant. I grew up in church my whole life and had been reading the Bible since I was a child, yet I couldn't really describe sanctification. I knew it had to be important because the Bible says, "Only he who does the will of the Father gets into heaven and his will is for you to be sanctified." It seemed to me that if I didn't understand sanctification, I probably wasn't doing it so that meant that I didn't qualify to get into heaven. That was a frightening thought. I did what anyone who hungered for the truth would do. I started searching the scriptures to learn about sanctification. Now there are some great teachers out there on this subject. I'm not one of them, but you will never really get it until you search it for yourself. The more I learned about sanctification, the more I realized that I had been living a lie most of my life. I had fallen victim to so many of the devil's lies and schemes because I was neglecting the most important process of my Christian walk. I was always compromising and holding on to a love for the world because I hadn't truly started the process of sanctification. It goes well beyond the sinner's prayer. The sinner's prayer is just the beginning of a process that will take a lifetime to complete. If we ignore this process, we're nothing more than Christians in the flesh, and that is unacceptable to God. What is this process of sanctification? Simply put, it's the process of becoming holy. God commanded, "Be holy because I am holy" (1 Peter 1:16 NIV). That's not a request, and it's not an option.

We are sanctified by the word, and if we're not in the word, we are not going through the process, which means we are out of God's will. Sanctification is accomplished only through the blood of Christ and the truth of his word. Holiness is not achieved by our works. A form of godliness won't work either. It doesn't matter how smooth a talker you might be, how much money you put in the plate, or what ministry you serve in. If it's not done out of love, it's just a show and a bunch of noise. Sanctification makes the difference, and it's one of the most important things we need to understand if we're going to be the hero God is looking for.

Some may think that I'm starting to sound legalistic. When someone brings up legalism to me, it's usually followed by "We are no longer under the old law. We are covered by grace." This is true, but it's not about rules, regulations, and law. It's not about what you consider to be a sin or someone else considers to be okay. Should Christians drink or not? Should Christians get tattoos? Is it okay for Christians to watch *The Walking Dead?* Can we please bring an end to all the petty controversies and get back to what's important? If you want to know what's right or what's wrong, then obey God and search out his word. Jesus saved us with every intention for us to be holy. Be holy because he is holy.

So who determines what holiness is? Does a certain denomination or doctrine? No. God does. God determines what is sin and what is right or wrong. When you stand before him in his kingdom on the Day of Judgment, he's not going to ask you what church you went to or how many friends you had on Facebook. He's going to open his own book to see if your name appears. If your name is not found in that book, you are lost for eternity. That's why it's important to be a student of his book here so your name can be in his book there. You will never understand his ways or his will if you don't read his word.

I'm not writing to stir up an argument of whether you can lose your salvation or if speaking in tongues is still done today. I'm writing this to point to one simple fact that God demands that we be holy and righteous—in his eyes and not man's. Holy and righteous because he is holy and righteous.

As you begin the process of sanctification, God will reveal to you what he considers holy and righteous, and that's discovered in his word and through prayer. God desires a unique and personal relationship with each of his creation. My experiences are probably going to be different from yours because your relationship will be personal to who God has created you to be. If your faith has been reduced to just attending church on Sunday and maybe helping in some form of ministry, you're missing out on some of the great things that God has to offer.

A real relationship with God should be exciting and even frightening at times. Why? Because to learning to trust him requires us to get out and walk where you wouldn't normally walk. Kind of like Peter walking on the water. He stepped out of the boat, took a few steps, and then what happened? His flesh got in the way. He took his eyes off Jesus and put them on the storm. He lost his focus and his belief that he could do it (Matthew 14:25–33 NIV).

We sink in this life when we take our eyes off the Father and focus on the world. We tend to put our focus on the world because for some reason we think the world dictates what is right and wrong, good and evil, and the standards by how a person will be judged and looked at. I've got news for you. God decides that, not man, and it's found in his word.

Paul writes in Romans 12:2 (NIV), "Do not to conform to the pattern of this world but be transformed by the renewing of your mind. Then you will be able to test and approve what God's will is—his good, pleasing and perfect will." There is a difference between stumbling and choosing rebellion. There are sins committed in weakness or ignorance, and there are sins we walk into knowingly. When we choose intentional sin, God disciplines us because He loves us. He does not do that out of cruelty, but out of fatherly love. If we belong to Him, then He calls us to a way of life that honors Him and strengthens His kingdom rather than tearing it down.

Nothing damages a witness faster than hypocrisy.

When someone claims to belong to God while regularly denying His Word through their lifestyle, the damage is real. Hypocrisy weakens testimony, confuses onlookers, and harms the work of the kingdom. It is one thing to struggle and repent. It is another thing to justify disobedience while still trying to wear the name of Christ.

The good news is that God does not command holy living and then leave us helpless.

On one of the so-called reality shows there was a young lady vying for the heart of the handsome single man. She was attempting to explain to him who she really was as a person. This was how she described herself.

"One minute, I might be on the front row at church on my knees weeping and worshiping God, and the next minute, I can be a devilish witch."

My first question would be "What exactly is being preached in that church?" If it's truth, then she obviously doesn't pay attention. But I see this a lot in the younger generation of Christians. One minute, they might be talking about the work they do in the church and how powerful Sunday service was, and the next, they are dropping more F bombs than the movie *Platoon.* By the way, scripture also tells us to let no unwholesome talk come out of your mouth (Ephesians 4:29 NIV). (Look it up.) If we call ourselves Christians, we represent him and the church. If the world can't tell us apart and accept us as one of their own, then we've taken God's name in vain, and I do believe that is the third commandment (Exodus 20:7 NIV).

Here's an interesting way to look at it. Think about each day that you live as if it were a movie. At the end of the day, rate your movie, or day. Was it rated R, PG-13, PG, or G based on what you said and how you portrayed yourself? You're the star in your own movie.

Who did you impact, or who did you cause to stumble? Did you offend anyone, and if so, in what way? There's a reason scripture tells us to keep our minds on things above and not on earthly things (Colossians 3:2). We must be aware of how we present ourselves daily because that is our witness. We were saved to come out of the world and not conform to it. We still love the sinner without condoning the sin so that we might have the chance to share the gospel with them.

There can be no room in our heart for hate. The process of sanctification removes hate, bitterness, anger, resentment, and everything that is the opposite of the fruits of the spirit. It doesn't happen overnight, but it does happen. We must be disciplined and persistent in our seeking of truth. We can't just go by how we feel. I have days when I feel God is nowhere to be found, but I know he is there because his truth tells me he is. Remember we are tested and tried to develop faith, trust, strength, discipline, and perseverance because as this world continues to grow more evil and the last days approach, we will need all these to stand strong against persecution and deception.

Only he who does the will of the Father will enter the kingdom. It is God's will that you be sanctified. We are sanctified by the word of God. Let your life be an everyday movie that glorifies God and not disgraces him. Don't be a stumbling block for others.

As for the question of whether or not Christians should drink, here's how I look at it. Whether it's a sin or not, I choose not to. And the reason I don't believe a Christian should condone it is because you never know when you might have a new convert who has struggled with alcoholism for years or a former drug addict in the congregation. You might have a former alcoholic at your little in-home Bible study and decide to break out the wine for a little social drink and Bible study. You've just become a stumbling block and created mass confusion for that person.

Again, Paul reminds us that even if something is permissible, it does not mean it is beneficial (1 Corinthians 6:12 NIV). We are washed and sanctified through Jesus Christ and should always consider others before ourselves. And using the verse that says to win the world, become like the world (1 Corinthians 9:22), which is not accurate by the way, doesn't work. I believe what the Bible is talking about here is respecting one's culture and way of life but without condoning their sins or bowing to their false gods.

I've traveled to many parts of the world, and by far India is the most interesting to me. When I would visit people's homes, I remove my shoes before entering and eat or drink what I'm given because that is their culture. But I do not pray to their Hindu gods, nor do I compromise my faith. I love visiting the people of India and have sat and had many deep discussions with some of the strongest Hindus, but I always treat them with respect and pray for them. Many will convert. I have a great story about that, but you'll have to wait a little bit more for that. Sorry.

Just keep this in mind as you read on. God is looking for heroes who are seeking truth and being sanctified by his word and the blood of Christ in order to become that one person who has the power to save an entire city. It can happen today, and you can be that hero. You just need to believe and seek the truth. Die to the flesh daily and follow Christ, and he will transform you into that hero to carry his message of salvation to those who need to hear it.

If we try to be that hero of faith, we will fail. We are not called to try to be Christian; we are called to be Christians. Not try to follow Jesus but follow Jesus. We are not to try to obey his word, but we are to obey his word. There is no trying to be holy, only being holy. Remember to be holy because he is holy. This is why so many fail, including me, because we allow ourselves this wiggle room with the word *try*. We provide ourselves with the option to fail. When it comes to following Christ, failure should not be an option. Either we are disciples of Jesus Christ or we are not. There's no middle ground when it comes to being a child of God.

He said, "You are either for me or you are against me." (Matthew 12:30 NIV). (Look it up.) The lamest excuse I constantly hear is "I'm going to fail anyway. At least we are covered by grace." You need a better understanding of grace and mercy. Dive headfirst into 1 John and see what the scriptures say about continuing to sin. The good news here is that if we do sin, we have an advocate to the Father who intercedes on our behalf. It's convenient to only remember the second part of that yet forget the first part that says *to not sin.*

We read just enough scripture or go to church just enough to give us a false sense of security without knowing that we are totally powerless. To be a hero of faith is to be dedicated to seeking truth and living it out daily, not just when it is convenient or feels right.

Chapter 4: Believing in What You Can't See

One thing I find troubling in our culture today is the fascination with death and darkness. Zombies have become a marketing empire, pulling in millions through television, movies, video games, and even children's toys. It is not just zombies, either. People are deeply curious about the dead, the paranormal, and the idea of communicating with spirits. Those themes show up everywhere now, and many people consume them without a second thought.

What is even more troubling is how many Christians treat those things as harmless entertainment. I do not believe they are harmless.

As we grow in sanctification, one of the things we must learn is to believe in realities we cannot see. Scripture tells us plainly that our struggle is not against flesh and blood, but against rulers, authorities, and spiritual forces of evil in the heavenly realms. If that is true—and I believe it is—then we should not be surprised that the enemy uses culture, media, and entertainment to blind people to truth and normalize darkness. Evil once tried harder to disguise itself. Now it often parades itself openly, and the uglier it is, the more attention it seems to get. If people could truly see what was behind some of what they celebrate, they would run to God instead of flirting with darkness.

I do not write that as theory.

I write it because I have seen enough to know that evil is real.

When I was a teenager, I had my first face-to-face encounter with something I could not explain away. I grew up in the 1980s, when people were already fascinated with hidden messages in music and with testing the boundaries of what they thought was harmless.

Music was a huge part of my life. It still is. Back then, there was not nearly as much to do, so I would sit in my room for hours listening to music and practicing guitar late into the night. I came from a musical family. My parents played, many relatives were gifted musically, and music was simply part of our home. The problem was that my taste in music was not always the same as theirs. They loved Southern and country gospel. I preferred mine louder and with a little more distortion.

I was raised in a Christian home. My father was a deacon, and church was not optional. We went, whether we felt like it or not. Looking back, I thank God for that. I had parents who loved us, worked hard, and raised us according to God's Word. We did not have a lot of money, but we had something far more valuable: a godly home.

When I think back on those years, one of the clearest memories I have is coming downstairs in the morning before school and seeing my dad sitting in his recliner reading his Bible. That image stayed with me. It taught me something no sermon alone could teach: faith has to be lived. It must be seen. It should be sought personally. Those moments are part of why I knew God was real. Before long, I would also learn that the devil was real.

Satan is not a cartoon character, a Halloween costume, or some invented idea meant to scare people into religion. He is real, and so are the powers of darkness that serve him. Scripture makes that plain. And as his time grows shorter, evil becomes more aggressive, more visible, and more normalized. That is why believers cannot afford to be careless. God is looking for people who will be sanctified, alert, and unwilling to compromise with a darkening world.

That truth became personal to me one night.

My parents were strict about music. There were some things I was allowed to listen to and some things I was not. They leaned toward gospel. I liked AC/DC, Mötley Crüe, Ratt, and the rest of that world. Since those were not welcome in the house, I kept some of that music hidden in my closet. Eventually I discovered Christian rock, and I loved it. To me, it felt like the best of both worlds: music I enjoyed without lyrics my parents had to worry about. My parents did not love it, but they allowed it. Some of it.

At the time, I thought the whole argument over music was exaggerated. I was a teenage boy, and naturally I knew more than my parents knew. Or so I thought. Looking back now, I understand that they were trying to protect the atmosphere of our home in ways I did not yet understand.

One night around two in the morning, I had been practicing guitar for several hours. My parents were asleep, so I pulled out some of the music I kept hidden and worked on a song until I was exhausted. When I was finished, I leaned my guitar against the amp beside my bed, turned off the light, and rolled over to go to sleep.

Just as I began to drift off, I had the unmistakable feeling that I was no longer alone in the room. My back was to the door, so I rolled over, expecting to reassure myself and see nothing.

Instead, I saw my black guitar floating in midair.

It was lying flat, just inches from my face. I stared at it in shock as it slowly drifted backward and settled again beside the amp where I had left it. No, drugs and alcohol were not involved. I know how that sounds, but I also know what I saw.

For a few moments, I tried to explain it away. I told myself I was tired. I told myself my imagination had gotten the better of me. Eventually I calmed down enough to lie back down again.

Then the feeling returned, stronger this time. I knew something was there.

I rolled over again, and before I could fully move, fear seemed to pin me in place. Hovering above me was not my guitar this time, but a face. There was no body. No arms. Just a large, burned-looking face hanging over my bed, smiling and laughing at me. It looked melted, hideous, and full of evil. The smile said everything:

I have you now. You're mine.

I could not look away.

Then it slowly drifted backward until it disappeared through the window.

That was all I needed.

This time, there was no trying to convince myself that it was my imagination. I was up and out of that bed and down the stairs, busting into my parents' bedroom door in record time. I don't think I touched a single step on the way down. Of course I freaked them out, but I was shaken up big time. After I had explained to them the events that occurred, they didn't react like most parents might have. They didn't try to convince me it didn't happen or it was all my imagination. No, my parents were spiritually wise enough to call the pastor, who arrived a little later with a couple other deacons.

When our pastor arrived, he felt the evil as soon as he walked through the door. They prayed through the house and made their way upstairs to my bedroom. When our pastor entered my room, he stopped in the middle of the floor and stood silently for a moment. He then turned toward my closet and said, "Whatever you have in that closet is the source of your problem." Uh oh. Busted. He walked over to my closet and, as if he had been there many times before, reached right into my hiding place and pulled out my bag of hidden goodies and dumped it all out on the floor.

Now understand I had no pornography, drugs, or anything else like that. Just music. My parents were standing with jaws wide open. I stood there even more confused because to me it was just music. Music that my parents didn't approve of and music that I had to hide to enjoy, but it was just music. Right? Read the story about King Saul and David and you'll discover the power that music has.

Joshua states in the Bible,

"But if serving the Lord is undesirable to you, then choose for yourselves this day whom you will serve, whether the gods your ancestors served beyond the Euphrates, or the gods of the Amorites, in whose land you are living. But as for me and my household, we will serve the Lord." (Joshua 24:15 NIV)

My parents declared this over our home, which meant that anything that didn't please the Lord had to go. If it didn't glorify God, it didn't belong. Please don't get the wrong idea about my parents. They were not religious nuts who tried to suck all the fun out of life. They understood things about the spiritual realms that I didn't.

And as my mother prayed, she felt led to go to my room. I had a case that held all my cassette tapes of the music that were mostly parent approved, and she began to pull certain tapes out and throw them away. She had the right idea but needed to walk about ten feet to the left and open the door to find what God was trying to lead her to. When I got home and saw she had thrown away some of my favorites, I was not happy. Later that night though, the truth was revealed.

As I reflected on that experience over the years, I came to believe that what happened was tied not only to the music itself, but also to my disobedience. Scripture commands us to honor our father and mother. My parents had dedicated our home to the Lord.

My father had declared, as Joshua did, that our house would serve the Lord. By hiding what they had forbidden and choosing disobedience, I had opened a door. The music was part of the doorway, but dishonor and rebellion were the key that turned the lock.

That was my first real encounter with darkness. It would not be my last.

My First Exorcism

Years later, after many mistakes and failures I will talk about more in this book, I came face-to-face with demon possession for the first time. When we commit ourselves to God's will, He sometimes leads us into places we never expected to go. That should not surprise us, because the Bible is full of moments that go far beyond ordinary human understanding. Still, when those moments come, they can shake you.

One thing I have learned is this: God does not send us into spiritual battles unprepared. He equips us over time. He teaches us. He develops discernment and dependence in us. If you rush into spiritual warfare under your own confidence, you can get yourself into trouble very quickly. Scripture gives a sobering example of that in the sons of Sceva. This is not something to approach casually.

I should pause here and say plainly that some of what follows may be unsettling. Not everyone believes in demon possession, and even many Christians avoid the subject entirely. Personally, I think that avoidance has cost the church dearly. Too many people say they believe the Bible while quietly dismissing the parts that make them uncomfortable. Ignoring darkness does not make it disappear. It only makes people easier to deceive.

At the time, I was working an overnight job delivering auto parts across Oklahoma and the Texas panhandle while also serving as a youth pastor. One night I was listening to a talk radio program that featured a priest discussing demonic activity and possession. It was creepy enough that I nearly changed the station, but something made me keep listening. As I did, I had a strong impression that I needed to begin studying and praying about spiritual warfare. I did not fully understand why, but I knew I was being prepared for something. That sense never left, so I began reading, studying, and spending time in Scripture on the subject. The Bible remained my main source.

About a year later, I got the call.

A close friend phoned in a panic and told me his wife was acting strangely and was not herself. He asked if I could pray for her. I told him to bring her to the church, and I called the pastor to meet us there. On the drive in, she had been speaking as though she were outside her own body, watching herself from the outside. By the time they arrived, it took all three of us to get her into the church. She was kicking, screaming, and fighting the entire way. I would be lying if I said there was not a part of me that wanted to run. But I knew I had to stay.

We brought her to the front of the church and held her down while the pastor rebuked the demon and commanded it to leave. As I watched, something unexpected began happening inside me. While the pastor was doing what he knew to do, I kept sensing impressions about how the battle should be handled. I do not say that to dishonor him. He was a good pastor and a good man. I simply knew I was being shown things in real time that I had not learned naturally.

After several intense minutes, she calmed down. She looked up at us and seemed unaware of where she was or how she had gotten there. The pastor then gave her good, biblical counsel about prayer, cleansing her home, and building a personal relationship with God. But even as he spoke, I sensed something unsettling: the spirits had not truly left. They had only gone into hiding. And I knew, somehow, that I would deal with them again.

A few days later, the next phone call came.

A woman from our church who had been mentoring this young lady asked me to come over because the young woman was overwhelmed by fear and deeply distressed. I knew before I got there what I was likely walking into. As soon as I hung up, I grabbed my Bible and hit my knees in prayer. That is the only way to walk into a battle like that. I was nervous enough to feel like a gladiator entering the arena, but I also knew God had been preparing me.

Before I left, I looked down at my watch. It had been a gift from my wife and kids and had a picture of Stevie Ray Vaughan on it. I felt strongly that I needed to take it off. The impression in my spirit was simple: do not give the enemy anything he can use against you. I cannot fully explain that, but I obeyed it. In spiritual battle, obedience matters, even when you do not fully understand why.

When I arrived, the young woman was sitting on the couch, clearly afraid. Her husband was there too, and I made small talk while waiting. I felt strongly that I needed to wait until he left. Once he did, it was time.

I opened my Bible and began speaking to her about the blood of Christ. She talked about fear, about being overwhelmed, about being tormented. The more I spoke about the blood of Jesus, the more agitated she became. Then, almost instantly, she changed. She bowed her head as if catching her breath, then looked up again—and it was obvious we were no longer dealing with the same presence. Her manner changed. Her expression changed. A different voice came out of her. At that moment I sensed clearly what I was to do: bind that spirit in the name of Jesus.

And the fear that had been knotted up inside me disappeared.

I looked her in the eye and commanded, “Spirit, I bind you in the name of Jesus.”

And the battle began.

Chapter 5:
The Fight for a Soul

There are moments in life when you realize just how small you are and how great God is. This was one of those moments.

It was one of those times when the Lord seems to say, *Do not fear. Be strong and courageous, because I am with you*—and then proves it.

I cannot fully explain where my fear went. One moment it had me tied up inside, and the next it was gone. In its place came a courage and authority I had never known before, not even in the military. What I do know is this: when I bound that spirit in the name of Jesus, it was no longer dealing with me alone. It was confronting someone infinitely greater and far more powerful.

For some time, I had sensed in my spirit that a moment like this was coming. But in my mind, I had imagined something much simpler. I thought it would be one spirit, one command, and one quick victory. Something like: bind it, cast it out, and move on.

That is not how it went.

If you study Scripture, you will notice that when God sends His people into battle, He often allows the odds to look stacked against them. He does that for a reason. When victory comes in a situation where human strength is clearly not enough, there is no confusion about who deserves the glory. The battle is won by His power, not ours.

As I confronted the spirits under the authority given to us through Jesus Christ, the first one to manifest was Fear.

Over time, I have come to believe that demonic spirits often reveal themselves in ways consistent with their function. Fear presented itself exactly that way. The voice, the demeanor, the torment—everything about it reflected fear and bondage. We all experience fear at times, but there is a difference between feeling fear and being ruled by it. Fear becomes destructive when it enslaves a person. And while not every struggle with fear means something demonic is at work, we do know that perfect love drives out fear.

When I commanded the spirit to identify itself, it answered, "My name is Fear."

I then asked whether Fear was the only spirit present. I expected a simple yes. Instead, I got a very clear no.

Fear then began naming the others, almost like a criminal turning in accomplices in hope of easing its own situation. Among the names it gave were Hate, Murder, and Liar. There were several in all, but those were the strongest. I assumed Hate was central because hatred feeds so much of what destroys people. To steal, lie, wound, or kill, hatred often takes root first. It can corrupt the mind, poison the heart, and separate a person from the peace of God. In that sense, Hate seemed like the strongest spirit in the group.

But Fear came first. That mattered.

Spirits that work together often strengthen one another, and the best way to weaken that kind of structure is to remove the weaker ones first. So after Fear had been dealt with, the next spirit to rise was Disobedience.

And Disobedience was exactly that—stubborn, defiant, and unwilling to yield. It refused to submit to the authority of Jesus Christ. It reminded me of a criminal resisting lawful commands at every turn. After repeated commands, I finally issued one last warning: if it would not obey the authority of Christ, I would call on my heavenly Father to deal with it directly.

That got its attention.

Disobedience screamed, then reluctantly gave way.

What felt like hours were only minutes. Eventually I bound the remaining spirits together and commanded them to leave in the name of Jesus—to go where they belonged and await judgment. For a moment, it seemed the battle might be over. She became calm and tried to act normal. She said she was fine and tried to pull away from us.

But I could see in her eyes that it was not over.

I commanded any remaining spirit to come forward and submit to the authority of Jesus Christ. That was when her body language changed again, this time becoming seductive in a way that made it obvious what we were dealing with.

The remaining spirit was Lust.

After a brief but real battle, that spirit too was cast out, and at last she was free.

One of the important things in a battle like this is understanding what gave those spirits a right to be there in the first place.

It is similar to a house. Someone does not usually enter unless they are invited or the door is opened to them. Sin works the same way. Scripture says it is crouching at the door, waiting. A person opens that door through choices, compromises, and invitations they may not fully understand at the time. Christ also stands at the door and knocks but evil does too. The question is always: which one are we opening the door to?

In this young woman's case, the doors had been opened mostly through drugs, a Ouija board, and witchcraft. The drug use was part of the invitation, and the occult involvement opened the door further. That may sound extreme to some readers, but I believe one of the greatest gateways to spiritual destruction today is drug use. If people truly understood how vulnerable they become through drugs and alcohol, many would think twice before touching them. The enemy comes to steal, kill, and destroy, and he is more than willing to use what many call harmless fun to do it.

One detail from that battle stayed with me afterward.

When I bound the spirits together, Lust did not leave with the others.

That bothered me, because I wanted to understand it. As I prayed, I sensed that certain spirits function together and can therefore be addressed together, while others operate differently and have to be confronted separately. Hate, disobedience, murder, and anger all seemed to function in one cluster, while lust had a different role and pattern. The best way I can explain it is this: if you walk into a room full of carpenters, electricians, plumbers, doctors, and nurses, you could group some together according to the work they do— but not all of them. Their functions are different. That is how I came to understand what had happened.

Here is what I know for certain: God deserves all the glory.

I would never attempt something like this casually, recklessly, or out of curiosity. I would never attempt it apart from prayer, preparation, and confidence in my relationship with God. I am grateful that He used me and grateful that this young woman was set free, but I did not enjoy this battle at all. I honestly hoped it would be one of those once-in-a-lifetime moments I could check off and never revisit.

It was not.

Not long after that, I learned something else that deeply affected me.

I had already said that drugs can be a gateway. But what if a drug is not just a chemical bondage in someone's life? What if, in some cases, it becomes something spiritually attached as well?

I came face-to-face with that possibility during a church service.

Remember how I talked about drugs being a gateway? What if I told you that a certain popular drug was a spirit and not just a drug? A woman who would attend our church from time to time often come up for prayer. She had a long history of drug abuse and would get into the cycle of getting delivered and then returning to it. That morning during altar call, she came up and sat down on the front pew. I walked over and began to speak with her to see what she wanted prayer for. She struggled to speak. It was as if an invisible hand was placed over her mouth.

I invoked the authority given to me through Jesus Christ and commanded her to speak. She would shake her head no and try to keep her mouth shut. After several minutes of struggling with the spirit, it finally spoke, revealing its name: Meth. She had become a prisoner of Meth again, but sadly, this time she was not ready to give up Meth.

She wasn't willing to renounce Meth and take away the rights the spirit had to her. One thing you can never do is force someone to give up a sin they love. They must make that choice on their own. Only God has the power to set a person free, but that person must want to be set free. You can't hold the hand of the devil and pray to God at the same time. The only thing we can do is pray that their eyes are opened to the truth and eventually surrender to God. It's heartbreaking, but that's the power of meth. It's so much more than a drug. It is a gateway to hell.

They Will Come Back

The Bible says that when an evil spirit comes out of a person, it goes through arid places, seeking rest, and does not find it. Then it decides to return to that person to see if their condition has changed. In other words, has the evil spirit been replaced with righteousness, and is the person being sanctified by the blood of Christ? If not, it not only returns but brings with it seven other spirits more evil than itself, and the condition of that person will be worse than before (Matthew 12: 43–45 NIV). (Look it up.) I learned the true meaning of this scripture through a familiar face.

Several years after my experience with my friend's wife and the spiritual forces of evil, I got the phone call I had always wished never to receive again.

I am always willing and ready to go face-to-face with evil, but I never look forward to it and that's a good thing. If I'm looking forward to it, then I risk losing my humility and may start relying on my own strength and ability. And that would be a disaster. I relate it to being a paratrooper, you hope and pray you never have to go to war, but if you're going, make sure you're prepared.

It was in the afternoon, and I was picking some things up at the store when I received the call from a dear pastor friend of mine. He explained to me that my friend's wife who God had delivered a few years earlier, was at his place and spirits were beginning to manifest during their conversation.

I wasn't sure how well she had been doing after her first deliverance. I knew she was doing well after a time and had some veteran Christians supporting her, but apparently she had went back to her old ways. In other words, her house was no longer being occupied with the things of God. The spirits returned and found the house empty and most certainly brought with them several spirits worse than the first.

My pastor friend described to me that she was being very erratic and the spirits were rotating, taking turns talking, and she wouldn't sit still. I agreed to go out to see if I could help.

When I arrived, she was pacing around the room. It was obvious by her demeanor that this battle was going to be at a much higher level and more intense than the last. She was not happy that I was there, and to be truthful, neither was I, but I wasn't about to back down. I knew entering this situation that God would take over and enable us to do what needed to be done, so I wasn't as nervous this time. We're simply the vessel that God uses to pour his strength and might into to deliver those bound by evil.

Pastor had been dealing with her for a while so I thought it best to allow him to continue and I would help him through it and support him. He would try to bind the spirits, but they were swapping places and eluding the attempts.

At one point, a spirit—I don't remember which one because there were so many—looked at me and called me by name. "I know you and all that you've done too."

I informed the spirit that I had been redeemed by the blood of the lamb, and this was not about me. I then commanded the spirit to give me its name, and I will never forget its response.

"We are a forest, and I'm the tallest tree." Immediately I thought of Legion from one of the four gospels (Matthew 5:1–20 NIV). Another scripture then came to mind. The one that says this kind can come out only by prayer & fasting (Mark 9:20). (Look it up.) If I understand correctly, the word fasting was added later and wasn't part of the original text. Either way, prayer and fasting go hand in hand, and when it comes to defeating the enemy, we need both. Jesus used both during his battle with Satan as he was being tempted.

Both are commanded, and both should be a regular part of our lives.

After realizing what we were dealing with, I began to pray in the spirit. Suddenly, it was as if an invisible blanket descended from above, so heavy that it drove me to my knees. I began praying more forcefully in an unknown language, as if my spirit was doing battle with hers. After praying intensely for a few minutes, I sensed her freedom as she prayed in the Spirit. She was clearly set free again, and her expression reflected it—a reminder that this is always a battle worth fighting.

I would hope that after that battle she would heed the advice of her pastor and not return to her old ways again. This is the same advice that everyone should adhere to when we come to know Christ. True repentance means we walk away from our old life. We die to sin and become slaves to righteousness.

Sin is what separates us from God, and if we think we can have a relationship with God while still living in sin, we are very mistaken. But there's a big difference in sinning through a moment of weakness and living in sin. Our new life should not look like our old one.

The old things pass away as we are renewed through Christ. Some things take time to change, but it's important we continue to seek truth and righteousness and not grow weary in doing good or becoming complacent. If we continue living in sin after receiving Christ, then the truth is not in us and we've accepted Christ in vain. Paul plainly instructs, "Stop sinning" (1 Corinthians 15:34 NIV).

I recently read an article by a well-meaning but very misinformed pastor. It stated that we don't need to confess and ask for forgiveness after every sin we commit. We've already been forgiven of all sins, past present and future, so there is no reason to ask for forgiveness again. My Bible tells me that if we commit a sin, then we need to repent of it. Sin is like a seed, and if it is left alone and not repented of, it will lead to death (James 1:13–15 NIV).

The problem with America today is not liberalism or what they are trying to accomplish in their socialist agenda. The biggest problem with America today is the number of people who claim to be followers of Christ but still live in sin. Many believe in him, but few truly follow him. There's a big difference in believing and following. Even the devil believes. It used to be that the word was the power to save and when led by the Holy Spirit, lives were healed and changed completely. The church has compromised so much with the world that now we are relying on fads, programs, and technology to do the work that God intended his word and spirit to do.

Many churches do a great job with bringing in crowds and building some very expensive and comfortable churches, but if you want to know who is following Christ and not just believing, remove it all, preach the truth, and see who stays. The most powerful services I have ever been a part of have been in our little church in India. It's a concrete building with a tin roof where you sit on the concrete floor, and it's about a hundred degrees inside with no breeze.

When we would do communion, I would be dripping sweat all over the bread I was passing around, but nobody noticed because they were worshiping in spirit and in truth. Not only that, but they would do this knowing that they were putting their lives on the line. Build a church like that here and see how big the congregation gets.

Earlier I had talked about my love for music and the style of music I enjoyed the most. The style of music that I loved that was once condemned is now played in modern worship. The question is this: was I wrong then or are they wrong now? I'm going to make this very simple for you. If you worship in spirit and in truth, you'll know what is pleasing to God and what is not. I've been in some services where the music was so loud, it was dark and the fog was so distracting there was no way I could worship in that atmosphere.

The singers and musicians were jumping around on the stage doing their best to put on a good show. To me, this is entertainment and not worship. Some may be able to worship in that atmosphere, but I'm not one of them. God saved me from a very dark place, and I don't really care to worship in darkness.

Ultimately, it's your actions that define you. Whether you worship in a church with booming music or prefer traditional hymns, these preferences are irrelevant unless you demonstrate righteous qualities—unless your life reflects the holiness and representation of Jesus Christ as intended by God. Our Savior said it himself. "For the mouth speaks what the heart is full of" (Matthew 12:34 NIV). Our words and actions will reveal to everyone else who we truly are, and our hearts will bear witness to the Father if we are his or not.

As for secular music, I look at it like this. I've heard a saying that music is food for the soul. We know that it is powerful and effective. It can take us back into time where we find ourselves meditating on the good old days, or it can get us pumped up for the big game or workout. If music is food for the soul, then consider some secular music as junk food.

The more we indulge in secular music, the weaker our spiritual man will become. The goal is to be transformed into the likeness of Christ, and for that to take place, we are not to love the things of the world and we are certainly not to compromise with it.

And it's not just music but television, movies, things we read, and things we do. All these will either have a positive or a negative effect on our spirit. And we know that if we walk in the spirit, we will not gratify the desires of the flesh (Galatians 5:16–18). (Look it up.) It's not about what we desire but what God desires. And just because something has a Christian label on it doesn't mean it's right. God gives us his spirit so that we can have discernment. We need this discernment when it comes to music or anything else we want to allow into our lives. Discernment is crucial when it comes to relationships. It doesn't matter if it's about dating or just friendship. We must be cautious of who we yoke ourselves to.

Think of it as two oxen yoked together to plow a field. They must be on the same page to accomplish what the farmer needs. If they can't work together, they will struggle against each other and fail to work the ground. The Bible says not to be yoked with unbelievers (2 Corinthians 6: 14–16 NIV). When we become his, he has a plan for us. The unbeliever will not have those same desires, and we will find ourselves struggling instead of getting the field harvested. It doesn't mean we can't have a friendship with unbelievers—that's how we win many to Christ—but it does mean we have to be cautious about those we call friends and especially brother.

During the last exorcism, I asked the spirit what right they had to possess her body again. I was told by the demonic spirit that one of her relatives—he even quoted his nickname—gave away the rights to the family during a ritual at the Masonic lodge. In other words, a generational curse had been put on the family through his membership with the Masons. Do not be yoked with unbelievers in any form or fashion, regardless of how appealing it may seem.

My son was having trouble with a friend and asked my advice on what to do. This person claimed to be a Christian, but their actions were anything but the actions and words of a Christian. I told him to think of it as if he were treading water and this person was a brick tied to his leg.

How long do you think you can tread water before the brick pulls you down and you drown? Not long.

If you want to live, you must cut the brick loose because God doesn't intend for us to just tread water but expects us to have the faith to walk on it. There are some relationships that we may need to cut loose, or they will drag us down with them. We can try to correct a brother and be an influence, but we can't allow them to become a stumbling block for us.

If you think that Satan has not infiltrated our churches in one form or another, think again. I was listening to a radio show one night and the radio host was interviewing a witch. She was the real deal. She had a love for Satan and devotion to him like many of us do for Jesus.

She was asked about the so-called white witches or good witches. Her response wasn't exactly what I was expecting. She said, "there's no such thing as a good witch. They are misguided and delusional and will burn in the same hell that I'm going to burn in. The only difference between me and the good witch is that I know I will face eternal damnation in a lake of fire, and I am okay with it."

I was having trouble believing what I was hearing. Here was a lady who believed in a place called hell and understood the torment she was going to face yet chose to follow Satan to hell because she had such a hatred for Christians.

She even said she took all the necessary steps to make sure her son didn't go to heaven. The radio host asked her what she did for a job as a witch and how she earned money. Her answer was that Satan provided her with everything she needed. She had a nice home and expensive cars. Pretty much anything she wanted she got. She was loyal to Satan, and he provided her with a luxurious lifestyle.

She was a very attractive woman, and Satan chose her to use her beauty against the church. She was the spirit of Jezebel in the flesh. Her task was to find a church and start attending the services like a new convert would. She would dress very modestly and blend in but still be very attractive. She took the time to get to know people, shed tears at the altar to blend in.

Over time, she would become active in the church, going to Bible studies and helping in different ministries, all the while watching the pastor. As the enemy, she would study his every move and interests to find what his weaknesses might be.

She would get a sense of whether he could be seduced, and if so, she would begin to implement her plan. This would go on for a long time and would begin with simple glances to catch his eye, and then maybe a friendly touch that was more like a caress.

If she got the response she was looking for, then she would increase her attempts and find moments when the pastor was at the church alone. Before he knew it, he would be receiving pictures of her in lingerie or even nude and she would slowly pull him into her web of seduction and have an affair that would eventually bring him down and destroy the church.

If the pastor was too strong, then she would choose a deacon. This was her calling and gifts from Satan, and she was happy to serve him, even knowing the consequences.

We have a saying in the army that translates perfectly to our walk with Christ. "Stay alert, stay alive." The only way we're invincible is when God goes to battle for us.

To be that hero of faith, we must realize that we are helpless and useless against evil without the power of the almighty Creator and the blood of Jesus Christ. Don't limit God's power by compromising with this world, and don't fall into the temptation to live the everyday commercialized Christian life.

We are not called to be man's idea of a Christian but God's, and we cannot know what that is until we get into the word. We are called and equipped to be so much more. We just can't allow the world to weaken us with its imitation religion that looks like Christianity but is far from the truth. If your walk with God is boring, or mundane, then you're not doing it right. Every day should be a new adventure in learning who God is and finding out who you are in him.

Steal, Kill, and Destroy

If it weren't for sin, there would be no need for heroes of faith. Because Satan is the author of evil and the emperor of sin, his influence brings about temptation and wrongdoing in the world. There is no goodness in him—he is the father of lies, always seeking to trick and deceive those who follow Christ. For example, Satan might whisper doubts into someone's mind or create circumstances that lure them away from God's truth.

That's why heroes of faith, like those described in scripture who overcame temptation and remained steadfast despite Satan's schemes, are so important; their courage and trust in God serve as examples for us all. If you take Satan lightly and underestimate his ability to deceive, you risk falling into his traps. Therefore, we must be vigilant and rely on our faith to resist his efforts to undermine our relationship with God.

Consider Adam and Eve: they walked with God and had a close, personal relationship with Him— something most of us can only imagine. Yet, even with this unique closeness, they still believed Satan's lie and chose to disobey. Adam and Eve's decision shows that temptation alone is not enough; ultimately, the choice to disobey was theirs. This story illustrates that while Satan can deceive and tempt us, he cannot force us to sin or compel us to choose wrong over right. The responsibility for our actions remains with us. Often, we make poor choices or are deceived because we allow ourselves to compromise with the world and, as a result, our faith becomes weaker.

For example, when we adopt values or behaviors that go against our beliefs just to fit in or gain approval, we risk distancing ourselves from God's truth and weakening our spiritual foundation. Satan persuaded a third of the angels to follow him, not by force, but through his skillful deception—he is, after all, an expert liar. In the same way, biblical figures like David, who fell into temptation with Bathsheba, or Peter, who denied Jesus out of fear, demonstrate that even the faithful can stumble when they yield to temptation. These stories remind us that resisting compromise and remaining steadfast in our faith is key to overcoming the enemy's lies.

Why do you think I keep telling you to look it up? Because your greatest weapon is found in the word—the teachings and scriptures contained in the Bible. It's not just about what someone else can teach you; it's about letting God's word come alive within you, revealing the truth of who God is and who He can be in your life. You are made perfect through Jesus Christ, and you can be more than a conqueror through the One who saves you. But if you don't experience the word for yourself—by reading and studying the Bible—you are simply trying to fight a war with no ammunition. You can't live an effective life of righteousness relying only on the hearsay or opinions of others. To actively engage, set aside time each day to read a passage from the Bible, join a study group to discuss scripture and share insights, and reflect on how these teachings apply to your daily life.

Your strength and power will not be found in any other speaker or pastor—it will only be found in Jesus Christ. While attending church and receiving good teaching is important, if you neglect the word of God yourself, you are setting yourself up for failure and defeat. Obedience to the word means following biblical principles in your daily life, striving to live according to God's instructions. Neglecting these teachings will only cause us to drift away from Him. Take ownership of your faith journey; be proactive, stay engaged, and allow God's word to transform your life.

Chapter 6: When God Speaks

To be a hero of faith, you must learn to listen for the voice of God and recognize it when He speaks.

Jesus said, "My sheep know my voice." That does not always mean an audible voice. For most believers, hearing from God is not like hearing thunder from heaven or a whisper in the ear. More often, it comes as a deep impression upon the heart and mind—something steady, clear, and consistent with His Word. That is one reason we are told to set our minds on things above rather than on the things of this world. The more we walk with Him, the more clearly we learn to recognize His leading.

I remember playing with Silly Putty as a kid. One of my favorite things to do was flatten it over a newspaper, lift it up, and see the image left impressed on it. It fascinated me.

In a simple way, that is how I think about the way God speaks to us. He impresses things upon the heart. His leading leaves its mark. And when it is truly from Him, it will always agree with His Word. As we seek Him and grow through sanctification, He has a supernatural way of guiding us into the center of His will without needing to say a single audible word. Our spirit responds to His Spirit, and then our bodies are called to obey.

Let me give you an example.

A Lunch Appointment I Didn't Plan

One day I was walking into a fast-food restaurant to get lunch when I noticed a homeless man sitting outside in the cold. He looked like he had been there a while, and people were walking past him as though he were invisible. As soon as I saw him, I felt the Lord impress upon me to bring him inside and buy him a meal.

So I did.

He was grateful just to be warm and have something to eat. When I sat down with the food, he asked if I was really sure I wanted to be seen eating with him. I told him yes. That conversation taught me again how foolish it is to judge by appearance.

The more we talked, the more I realized there was much more to this man than what people would have assumed at a glance. He was intelligent, thoughtful, and articulate. He carried a small pencil box with just a few possessions and some written reflections from his journey. When I asked how he had become homeless, he told me he had once held a highly technical job in New Mexico, enjoyed the good salary, the nice cars, and the comfortable life—but left it behind because he became convinced there had to be more to life than possessions and status. He had chosen to walk across the country instead.

That lunch was a reminder that obedience to God often begins with very simple acts. You do not always get a dramatic assignment. Sometimes He simply tells you to stop, see someone, and love them like they matter.

And they do.

In the Lion's Den

I have had several moments like that throughout my life, but one of the most intense happened while I was working in a maximum-security prison. It was one of the hardest jobs I ever had. The place was understaffed, volatile, and dangerous. I prayed constantly for God to open another door, but every time I did, I sensed the same thing: stay faithful and trust Him. Later, I found out why.

One evening I was in a pod while inmates were out of their cells preparing for dinner. The officer in the tower above was supposed to be watching us and buzzing the door when it was time for me to come out. But dinner was delayed, tensions were rising, and he was not paying attention. Before long, chairs were being thrown and profanity filled the room. I was waving my arms, trying to get his attention so I could get out, but he never even noticed. I was standing in the middle of a potential riot when I noticed one inmate in particular and I felt God impress upon me to go to him.

That was not an assignment I wanted. The man was large, furious, and exactly the kind of person I would have preferred to avoid in that moment. But I could not shake the impression, so I walked through the chaos and approached him with no real plan for what I was going to say.

I simply told him, "I know you're upset, and I know you don't get treated with much respect, but I want you to know that I genuinely care about you guys."

I was not prepared for what happened next.

His eyes filled with tears, and he told me that he and his wife had prayed the day before that God would send someone into that prison to show him that God still cared and that at least one person would treat him like a human being. Right there in the middle of the chaos, we were both crying. For a moment, it was as if everything else around us disappeared.

That moment taught me something I have never forgotten: being a hero of faith often means following God into places that feel uncomfortable, dangerous, or inconvenient. But those are often the very places where someone is waiting for an answer to prayer. If we listen and obey, God will take care of the rest.

And those are the moments that matter most.

Not the compliments after a sermon. Not the praise that comes from being seen. The moments that matter are the ones where a soul is touched, a person is encouraged, someone is led to Christ, a hurting child is healed, or a forgotten person is finally treated with dignity. Those are the moments a hero of faith lives for.

Dreams and Visions

God speaks to us through his word first and foremost, but he also impresses things upon our hearts and reveals things to us through his Holy Spirit. He also communicates with us through our dreams and visions. God spoke through the prophet Joel concerning the last days, saying, "I will pour out my spirit on all people. Your sons and daughters will prophesy, your old men will dream dreams, your young men will see visions" (Joel 2:28 NIV). This passage highlights that God's communication through dreams and visions is not just a thing of the past, but something He continues to do today. Throughout the Bible, figures like Joseph and Daniel received important messages from God through dreams, showing that this form of communication has a long history in scripture. These examples underscore how God uses dreams to guide, warn, and encourage his people, both then and now.

Not all dreams have a particular meaning some are simply dreams that fade from memory. However, I've learned that when God is trying to tell you something through a dream, it is usually very realistic, unforgettable, and carries a strong emotional or spiritual impact. For example, dreams that seem especially vivid, carry a strong emotional weight, or are accompanied by a sense of urgency may be worth prayerfully considering as possibly significant. It may be hard to determine the meaning, and sometimes the answer takes time to be revealed, but it's important to write such dreams down and pray about them. Have you ever had a dream that felt especially significant or memorable? Consider writing it down and asking God for insight into its meaning. Here's an example.

One night, I had a dream that seemed so real I could almost taste the cool air and feel the damp earth under my boots. An old army buddy showed up, his voice familiar and steady, asking if I could help him with something urgent. I immediately agreed—he was the kind of friend I would trust with my life. I remembered a night years before when, during a tense patrol in hostile territory, he pulled me out of harm's way just seconds before an explosion erupted nearby. That memory echoed in my mind, reinforcing my loyalty and trust in him now.

As we moved through the night, the world felt heavy and tense. Moonlight flickered across our camouflage as branches scraped my hands, the scent of wet leaves and distant smoke filling the air. The only sounds were our boots crunching on gravel and the soft rustle of our gear. When he instructed me to carry my weapon, a chill gripped my spine—I trusted him, but the urgency and secrecy unsettled me. We arrived at a tall fence enclosing a compound, its metal cold and slick beneath my palms as we climbed over, adrenaline coursing through me. Inside the sprawling concrete bunker, the scent of oil and gunpowder was overwhelming. Shadows danced on stacks of ammunition and missiles. He frantically grabbed rifles, whispering we only had a few minutes before they would catch us. My anxiety surged, confusion gnawing at me as the situation spiraled out of control.

Suddenly, sirens blared, piercing the silence. Bright lights flashed around us, painting the room in frantic red and white. My heart pounded with confusion and fear, and I couldn't understand why my friend had led me into this situation. Betrayal stung deeper than any wound as the chaos unfolded. I could feel sweat trickling down my neck, my mouth dry with panic, my senses sharp and overwhelmed and then I woke up, breathless, still grappling with the shock and loss.

The dream felt incredibly real, and I was certain it was a message, though I couldn't decipher what it meant at first. After spending several days praying about it, the dream lingered in my mind, refusing to fade. Finally, clarity settled in—I sensed deep within my spirit that the dream was a warning about a friend who would betray me. That realization left me unsettled, and I found myself constantly questioning which of my friends it could possibly be. The next evening, I was spending time with a good friend—someone I trusted deeply— joking around like we always did. Hoping for some understanding, I decided to tell him about my dream.

When I finished recounting it, he looked at me and asked if I understood what it meant. I admitted my suspicion that it might be about a betrayal by someone close to me. In that moment, I caught a flicker of guilt and pain in his expression, and I knew, with a sinking heart, that he was the one. A wave of disbelief, hurt, and sadness washed over me; it felt as if a part of my trust and the foundation of our friendship had been shattered. I wanted to deny it, to dismiss the possibility, but deep down, the truth was undeniable. My heart ached with a mix of sorrow and betrayal, and I remember feeling lost—like the ground had given way beneath me.

Two days after that conversation, I received a phone call that confirmed everything. The caller told me exactly what my friend had done—and had been doing—and suddenly all the pieces fell into place. My friend called, trying to explain himself and twist the story, but thanks to God's warning in my dream, I was able to listen with clarity and keep my guard up. The pain of betrayal was still there, but I was grateful that the dream had prepared me; otherwise, I might have dismissed what I was being told and let myself be blindsided. Instead, I was able to face the truth, even though it hurt, holding onto the comfort that God had been looking out for me.

God has used several dreams to teach me, warn me, and show me his will for my life. Sometimes we get so caught up in other things that our dreams are the only time he can get through to us.

I had another dream that I believe to be an end-time dream.

I was in an upper room of the White House. I've never been in the White House, so I have no idea what it looks like except for what I've seen on television and in books, and that was mostly of the Oval Office. I'm not sure if I was in the Oval Office or not, but I was surrounded by several other people. I noticed that it was people of all races, men and women, and I believe even some children. The scene was like the description in the Bible of how the Holy Spirit came down on the disciples in the upper room. The Holy Spirit had come down like tongues of fire on all the people in the room, and everyone began speaking in an unknown language. It was so powerful and real. I didn't recognize any of the people. I just remember it was a very diverse group and we were united in one spirit and in truth.

As we continued to pray, I became distracted by a whistling noise. At first it was subtle, but it grew louder and louder. I made my way to the window overlooking the yard of the White House and looked up into the sky. As the whistling sound grew louder, I could see something in the distant sky that was coming closer and closer and growing larger. It was a missile. The last words I spoke were "Jesus, I'm ready to come home." The missile struck directly at the center of the flagpole where Old Glory was flapping in the wind.

This was by far the most realistic dream I have ever had. So realistic that I felt the percussion from the blast. I lay there in my bed in the dark while thinking, Is this what heaven looks like? It's so dark and cold. It took me a few seconds to come out of it and realize that it was a dream and I was still in my bed in a dark and cold room.

I believe this dream holds deep spiritual and prophetic significance, which is why I see it as an end-time dream. The diverse group gathered together in unity reminds me of Acts 2:17, where God promises to pour out His Spirit on all people in the last days. The unity among people of all backgrounds in the dream symbolizes hope—that in times of crisis, faith can bring us together beyond our differences. The missile, to me, represents an impending crisis or judgment, a sudden event that could change everything in an instant. Yet even as danger approached, our focus was on prayer and on God, showing that our response to uncertainty must be to seek Him together. The dream seems to say that while trouble may come, unity in prayer and faith is our strength and our hope.

After waking up, I felt a lingering sense of urgency and gratitude for each day. The emotional impact of the dream stayed with me, reminding me to cherish the unity of believers and to remain spiritually prepared, no matter what may come. It also challenged me to look beyond divisions and to value the presence and voices of people from all walks of life. Even now, I find myself reflecting more deeply on the importance of prayer, faith, and unity—especially in uncertain times.

What do I think this dream is trying to say? I believe it echoes the message of Acts 2:17, where God promises to pour out His Spirit on all people in the last days. While this outpouring is available to everyone, I recognize that not all may be open or willing to receive it. My intention in sharing this is not to be political, but rather to reflect on the spiritual implications I sense. For example, President Trump has, in my view, taken notable steps to support Christians and give our faith a greater presence in national discussions. He has also drawn attention to issues of hypocrisy and moral challenges within the political sphere, and I see this as significant for people of faith.

While I know many people have different views on President Trump's actions and legacy, I have personally witnessed efforts that I believe have brought Christian values and discussions about faith back into the public arena. I recognize that no leader is perfect, and President Trump himself has acknowledged his own flaws and history. Still, from my perspective, his administration's support of religious freedom and friendship toward Israel have been meaningful. At the same time, I am deeply concerned that some policies and cultural trends in our country do not prioritize the sanctity of life or uphold the values I hold dear. These are complicated issues, and I understand that sincere people may disagree, but I believe it is important for Christians to continue standing for truth, life, and faith amid challenging times. This is not a season for lukewarm commitment; rather, I feel called to a deeper faith and unity, encouraging all believers to seek God's wisdom and respond to current events with courage, compassion, and hope.

With the unborn child becoming the human sacrifice to Baal through abortion and the war on genders, I wanted to understand how anyone could be so blind to follow something so evil? I find myself studying the book of Romans. How God had warned the people repeatedly to turn from their evil ways but as they continued to reject God, he finally gave them over to their sinful minds and desires until their hearts became hardened.

They chose to trade truth for a lie. A lie that would please their flesh and give them the evil desires that they hungered for. We see the same thing going on today. It boggles the mind how anyone could agree to the killing of an innocent child, even after birth, yet they continue passing laws not only allowing it but celebrating it.

This world is going to end, and if you're not for God, you are against God. Being a lukewarm Christian is certain death and damnation for eternity. To choose this world over God makes us an enemy to God. (James 4:4 NIV). (Look it up.)

We have the LGBT movement and transgenderism, which is a clear abomination to God but is nothing new. These things were going on long before America existed. Study the apostle Paul's letters to the churches, especially the church in Corinth. The city of Corinth also had a nickname. It was called Sin City.

Sound familiar?

The people of the city would go to their false gods and worship them through sexually immoral acts. Paul was warning the Christians in Corinth that they could not participate in such activities as followers of Jesus Christ. These practices began to make their way into the church, and Paul condemned them for it.

It's important to note here that Paul was not just condemning homosexual acts but all forms of sexual immorality. Watching or participating in any sexually immoral acts is forbidden by God. Nothing irritates me more than to hear a professing Christian condemning the homosexual community while they have an addiction to porn. Sexual immorality is an abomination to God in any form, not just homosexuality. Remember you will be judged by the standards that you hold others too (Matthew 7:2 NIV). (Look it up.)

Committing Our Work to God

Commit to the Lord whatever you do, and he will establish your plans.

Proverbs 16:3 (NIV)

When we're trying to decide on a career path we should take, hearing from God and following him is essential. Committing our work to Him means focusing less on what we want to do and more on what God wants us to do. If we trust Him and seek Him with all our heart, He will establish our steps and move heaven and earth to place us where He desires. Let me share how this principle played out in my own life.

My wife and I were serving as youth pastors in a small church in Oklahoma. We loved the church and were loved and treated very well—they truly spoiled us. But when I made my commitment to God, it was to go and do whatever He wanted, regardless of when, where, or how. I always trusted that He would make a way. Eventually, when it was time for me to move on to the next phase God had prepared, I began to feel restless and sensed a shift in my spirit. This feeling didn't come from the people around me, but from somewhere deeper. I found myself increasingly unsettled, prompting me to spend more time in prayer and reflection. Through these moments, I gradually understood that God was preparing me for something new. As I sought His direction, I would start asking God what was next, confident that He would lead me forward.

I was beginning to feel that it was time for me to resign and move on. This was a very difficult decision for me to make, and I wasn't about to make it hastily and without an assurance that it was God's will. The last thing I wanted to do was hurt the church and the pastor, but I knew I had to be obedient. This weighed on me so much that when praying about it, I asked God to show me in a dream what I was to do.

After all, he had revealed things in dreams before and this would be a great opportunity for him to do it again. So I went to sleep that morning because I was working nights in anticipation of having a dream that was going to reveal God's grand plan. I woke up disappointed. No dream. No revelation. Nothing. I was just as confused as I was when I had gone to sleep.

As I began sensing that my time at the church might be ending, an overwhelming mix of emotions washed over me. The thought of resigning was almost paralyzing this community wasn't just a place of worship but had become like family. My loyalty to the congregation and the pastor ran deep, and the idea of causing them pain or disappointment weighed heavily on my heart. Yet, amid that loyalty, there was a persistent, quiet urging in my spirit, nudging me toward something new—something I couldn't yet see but felt called to trust.

Faith has always been a guiding force in my life, especially when the path ahead is unclear. In past seasons of uncertainty, I'd found reassurance through prayer and even dreams, moments when God had spoken to me in ways so personal I couldn't deny His leading. Those experiences had taught me to seek His will above my own desires, leaning in for comfort and direction when I felt lost or afraid.

Faced with this new crossroads, I desperately wanted that same unmistakable clarity. My prayers became more fervent and vulnerable, honest confessions of my confusion and longing for guidance. I even asked God to speak to me in a dream, as He had before, hoping for a sign that would make the next step obvious. After a restless sleep, I awoke with no vivid dream, no revelation just the same uncertainty gnawing at me.

That silence was deeply disappointing. I found myself questioning whether I was missing God's voice or if I simply needed to wait in faith a little longer. What made this decision so difficult wasn't just the fear of change or the unknown, but the tension between honoring commitments and following the gentle, persistent call of the Holy Spirit. In those vulnerable moments, I realized again that faith often means stepping forward without all the answers, trusting that God's guidance may come in unexpected ways, and believing that He would not let me miss the way if I kept seeking Him.

Later that day, I received a phone call from my sister. The first words out of her mouth were, "I had a strange dream about you." She proceeded to tell me that in her dream I was standing in front of my pastor in a suit and telling him that it was time for me to go. Then she asked, "Does this make any sense to you?"

My first thought was, Next time I ask God for something, I need to be more specific. I had asked God to show me in a dream but didn't say whose dream. The realization hit me with a mixture of relief, awe, and even a little nervousness. I knew exactly what it meant; God had answered my prayer in a way I hadn't expected. While I felt affirmed in my decision, I was also anxious about leaving behind a community I cared for deeply and stepping into the unknown. The transition was filled with moments of doubt and struggle, but I chose to move forward, trusting that obedience would lead to growth.

Just as my sister's dream guided me, we are often called to trust God's direction even when it's difficult, knowing that each phase serves a greater purpose. God moved us to the next phase in life to prepare us for the phase after that. If you're a disciple of Jesus Christ, your eyes should always be focusing on things above and working toward that next phase—not because it's going to benefit you, but because the kingdom will benefit from it and others will be saved. Every phase we go through is not always pleasant, but they are designed to increase our faith and teach us to know the will of God.

My other example had to do with my job. I had a good job making good money, and on the surface, there was no reason to leave the stability and security it offered. But then a friend approached me about going into business with him. The idea was exciting—I really liked what he proposed, and I had every reason to trust him. As I considered his offer, I began to seriously weigh the risks and rewards. On one hand, I valued the steady income and the familiarity of my current position; on the other, the prospect of building something new with a close friend, the potential for greater growth, and a deeper sense of fulfillment drew me in.

I thought about what mattered most to me—being challenged, working in an environment of trust, and the possibility of making a greater impact. After praying about it and reflecting on my priorities, I believed this was a great idea and was ready to take the leap. I told my friend that I was in and was very excited for the new adventure. He was going to get the ball rolling and let me know when it was time to go to work. I had even gone so far as to talk to my current boss about the change and gave him a notice that I would be leaving when everything was in place. It was taking a while to get all the paperwork in order, so I hadn't heard from him much, but I eagerly waited for that phone call.

Then one day, I was on my way to work, and as I was driving down the street, God impressed upon me that I was going to hear from my friend that day and I was to tell him that I couldn't do it. This really confused me because I was excited about it and thought that it was God's will for me. But these instructions were pressed on me pretty hard. I decided that if this was really God, then I would hear from my friend soon. Later that morning, just as I was settling into my routine at work, I received a phone call from him asking me if I was ready to go to work. I was a little shocked and surprised, as you might guess, but I remembered what God had impressed upon me—or I guess you can say the Holy Spirit spoke to me. I told him that as much as I wanted to, I wasn't supposed to. I had to be obedient to God, and with him being a good Christian man, he understood that completely.

Looking back, it turned out that the move would not have been a good one for me, and I would have missed out on God's real plans for my life. For example, I later learned that the job was unstable and would have required me to relocate far from my support system—something that would have put a strain on my family and spiritual life. I think sometimes we let our fantasies take on the appearance of God's will and in doing so move out of his true will for us. If we will commit our work to him, then he will establish our plans and put us where he needs us. I've done my best to go and do whatever he asks of me, and I have found myself in positions that I probably didn't deserve or weren't even qualified for. But God works in mysterious ways and we are not to question him—just obey him.

Have you ever faced a moment when following your intuition or faith led you down an unexpected path? Trusting in something greater can sometimes mean letting go of our own plans.

If you're finding yourself in a dead-end job and you're miserable, try looking at the job through the eyes of God and seek him. If you're supposed to be there, you'll gain an understanding of why. If you're committing your job to him, then he will open new doors for you if that is his will. Sometimes he keeps us in positions that we struggle in so that we can learn perseverance and discipline. At the same time, whether you draw strength from your faith, personal values, or a sense of responsibility to others, reflecting on your role can help you find meaning and growth even in difficult circumstances.

The hardest thing to do is find the good and see people the way that God sees them when you're miserable, but you can start by identifying one positive aspect of your job each day or looking for small ways to support your coworkers. These actions can help shift your perspective and make your work experience more meaningful. If we're miserable at our job, maybe it's because we haven't committed it to him yet—or perhaps the challenge lies in our perspective or engagement. By taking intentional steps, you may discover new purpose and fulfillment, regardless of where your motivation comes from.

Navigating a workplace filled with negativity and bitterness can feel overwhelming, but this is exactly where our faith calls us to stand out. Think of it this way: there's a big difference between being a thermometer and a thermostat. A thermometer simply reports the temperature—it reflects whatever atmosphere surrounds it, whether that's frustration, gossip, or discouragement. In contrast, a thermostat has the power to set the temperature; it intentionally changes the environment, raising or lowering it as needed. As followers of Jesus Christ, we are called to be thermostats—agents of positive change who respond to negativity with kindness and hope, shifting the entire mood of a room.

For example, imagine a meeting where coworkers begin to complain about a difficult project. Instead of joining in, you might steer the conversation toward solutions, acknowledge the team's strengths, or suggest ways to support each other. By starting constructive discussions, you help redirect the group's energy from defeat to determination, gradually transforming the atmosphere. Consider this scenario: When a wave of gossip sweeps through the break room, you gently shift the topic—perhaps by highlighting a coworker's recent accomplishment or sharing a story about teamwork. In doing so, you break the cycle of negativity and set a tone of encouragement, showing that it's possible to be a thermostat rather than just reflect what's around you.

The key to consistently influencing your workplace for good lies in daily commitment to seeking God—not just during tough moments, but every single day. When we bring our jobs, families, and lives before Him, God grounds us in His purpose and empowers us to grow right where we are. As you approach each day with intention, pay attention to your reactions and the example you set for others. Choose to listen for God's guidance and follow His lead; He will never steer you wrong. Remember, change begins with one person—let that person be you, setting the temperature for faith and positivity wherever you go.

Chapter 7:
The Link to Hope

As Christians, we are more than just representatives of truth and righteousness. We are also a link—a link to a hope that many people in this world have never truly experienced. Through Christ, we hold the message that frees people from hopelessness, and to keep that message to ourselves goes against everything Jesus died for. Scripture tells us that God comforts us so that we can comfort others who are walking through affliction.

What He gives us is never meant to stop with us.

I first began hearing the phrase "Link to Hope" after my daughter recovered from her first battle with cancer. At the time, I assumed it had something to do with a ministry for families going through the same kind of pain and uncertainty we had just endured. We tried a few things. We made some trips to the hospital, offered encouragement, and looked for ways to minister to others in similar situations. But like many efforts that begin with passion and little clarity, it did not last long. Even so, we never stopped trying to encourage people when the opportunity came. My wife was especially gifted in that. She could minister to hurting mothers in ways I never could, and she was a blessing to many.

After a few years, life settled back into its normal routines. We stayed involved in ministry through our local church and community, and for a while it seemed that season had passed. Then Ashley's cancer came back.

This time it was in her lung, and suddenly we found ourselves back in that nightmare no parent ever wants to revisit. Another year of chemotherapy. More hospital stays. More uncertainty. More pain. Yet even in that season, my daughter and my wife were both incredibly strong. Ashley kept fighting, and my wife kept standing.

By then, my response was different too. The first time, I reacted in anger and confusion. This time, I immediately began asking God, what are You trying to teach me now? And once again I began hearing that phrase: Link to Hope. I knew there was more to it, but I still did not understand what.

At that point, I decided the next step must be to finish the schooling I needed for my ministerial license with the Assemblies of God. In my mind, I had already started to build the picture of what this calling would look like. I assumed I was going to become an evangelist. We would create a ministry called Link to Hope Ministries, travel around, preach, and watch God open doors everywhere. It all made perfect sense to me. Or so I thought.

A good friend invited me to preach at his church in New Mexico, and I went there full of expectation. The service was powerful. God moved in a remarkable way, and I left convinced that I had found my lane. I was sure this was it. I was going to be an evangelist, travel widely, and do big things for God. I can laugh at that version of myself now.

I did everything I thought an evangelist was supposed to do. I built a website. I started promoting myself. I prepared for the calls to start pouring in. In my mind, it was only a matter of time before the calendar filled up and the ministry took off. But that is often how we are.

When God gives us a glimpse of purpose, we are quick to build a plan around it. We interpret His call through our own preferences, ambitions, and assumptions. We imagine the platform. We picture the role. We decide what success will look like. And many times, we do it before God has fully spoken.

What I have learned since then is that calling is not the same thing as ambition. A true calling from God is not about building a name for ourselves. It is about making His name known. It is not about becoming impressive. It is about becoming obedient. God may call one person to preach to crowds, another to pray faithfully in secret, another to encourage broken families in hospital rooms, and another to love one hurting person at a time. The assignment may not look impressive to the world, but if it is from God, it matters eternally.

That is what the phrase Link to Hope was really teaching me. Hope is not a brand. It is not a slogan. It is not a ministry strategy. Hope is a person. Hope is found in Jesus Christ. And if we belong to Him, then our job is to become a living connection between hurting people and the hope only He can give. Sometimes that happens through preaching. Sometimes it happens through prayer. Sometimes through a conversation in a hospital hallway, a word of encouragement to a weary parent, or simply showing up for someone who feels forgotten. The method may change, but the mission does not.

We are called to connect people to hope. That also means God often uses our deepest pain as preparation for our future ministry. The comfort He gave us through Ashley's suffering was never meant to stay locked inside our own story. It was meant to become something we could carry to others. Pain has a way of opening our eyes to the suffering around us. It humbles us. It softens us. It teaches us how to recognize brokenness in others. And if we let God redeem that pain, it becomes part of how He equips us to serve.

I did not understand that at first. I thought the goal was to figure out the ministry title, build the platform, and move forward. But God was after something deeper than that. He was shaping my heart. He was teaching me that ministry is not ultimately about position, visibility, or even certainty. It is about obedience.

He reveals things in stages. He teaches us a little at a time. And many times, what we think is the destination is only the beginning of the lesson.

What does it mean to be a link to hope? It means living in such a way that people can find Jesus through your life. It means letting God use your wounds, your story, your faith, and your obedience to help someone else keep going. It means understanding that what God brings you through is often meant to become part of what you offer to others. And it means refusing to turn calling into self-promotion.

The world is full of people who are hanging by a thread.

Some are sick. Some are grieving. Some are addicted. Some are afraid.

Some are angry at God.

Some are smiling on the outside while quietly losing hope on the inside. What they need is not another polished performance. They need a real connection to the hope of Christ. That is what we are called to be.

A link to hope for others.

My Link to Hope Revealed

I was sitting one evening praying and studying the word when I came across a scripture that read, Religion that God our Father accepts as pure and faultless is this: to look after orphans and widows in their distress and to keep oneself from being polluted by the world (James 1:27 NIV). I had read this same verse many times before, but this time was different. It pressed on me hard.

What first caught my attention was what God considers to be the purest religion. When you are trying to follow Jesus and be in the will of God, knowing what He considers to be true religion is very important.

The next part got me though: to help orphans and widows in their distress. I lived in a very small town and didn't really know of any widows in distress nor were there any orphanages. As I sought God for guidance, I felt both excited and anxious—sensing a calling but unsure where it might lead. Each day, I wrestled with questions and doubts, hoping for a sign or some clarity. I knew He was trying to tell me something, but I didn't know what I was supposed to do with this new revelation.

Then I met a man named Syam, and God swung the door wide open to a new ministry in a country far away. But before I share how meeting Syam changed everything, let me take you back to the early 1990s, just after the first Gulf War, to provide important context.

I served with the 82nd Airborne Division in Saudi Arabia and Iraq during Operation Desert Shield/Desert Storm. We'd been away from home for months, spending our days living and training in the desert before the war began. Everyone was exhausted and homesick—we just wanted the conflict to start so it could end, and we could finally return home. I missed my wife terribly. After witnessing how difficult it was for my friends who had children, I felt grateful that my wife and I hadn't started a family yet. Even just being apart from her was hard enough.

When hostilities commenced, our forces advanced toward the Iraqi border to initiate operations against Saddam Hussein's Republican Guard. The United States Air Force launched an initial bombing campaign that targeted fortified defensive bunkers utilized by the Republican Guard. After crossing the border, significant casualties and structural damage were evident. Survivors of the air strikes were generally willing to surrender and be taken into custody, many of whom appeared to be suffering from hunger. The level of fortification in the bunkers did not meet expected standards for such defensive positions.

The war progressed much faster and more smoothly than we had anticipated, at least until the cease-fire was announced. When the cease-fire came, we felt immense relief—finally, it seemed possible to go home and reunite with our loved ones. Our staging area was set up inside what appeared to be an abandoned rock quarry encircled by a chain-link fence. While waiting for orders to begin packing up and preparing our equipment to return home, our unit stayed there. Before the cease-fire, we had taken several prisoners, collected their weapons, and handed them over to be processed.

After the cease-fire, the order came down to release our prisoners but keep their weapons. We had a pretty good stack of AK-47s that we had gathered from the Iraqi soldiers and kept in a small building within our fence. We released any prisoners that we had and sent them on their way. The cease-fire was in effect so there shouldn't have been any trouble. They had been fed and taken good care of, and most seemed grateful for the care and respect that we had given them. But within a few days of releasing these prisoners, we would find out that this was a terrible mistake.

There was a small village just a couple of miles up the road from us. Many of the people of that village would come out to where we were stationed and visit with us. We would give them food and do our best to have a conversation, but the language barrier made that very difficult. Yet it was very clear that they were grateful for us being there and what we had done for them. They were so friendly, and I couldn't help but love these locals.

I had one man who had approached me for some food, so I had given him a case of MREs. I was sick of them anyway. He left very thankful. He was so thankful that he returned later with his daughter, who looked to be about sixteen or so, and handed her to me while saying, "You keep. You keep." I must admit this caught me off guard, and I wasn't sure how to respond to this. Who would give their daughter away for food? First, military food does not hold that much value. Second, how in the world would I explain this to my wife back home? Luckily my platoon daddy was there to help explain to this gentleman that I couldn't keep her and that he didn't owe us anything for the food. I loved these people and their strange culture. But these same people we had befriended would soon be fighting for their lives.

The Iraqi soldiers we had released began to regroup in the area, particularly in the village up the road. They had obtained rifles, knives, swords—anything that could be used as a weapon—and began terrorizing the village and killing the innocent. I would not have believed that this level of brutality and evil was possible if I had not been there myself. These people who had become friends were now fleeing for their lives from a war that was supposed to be over.

Our commander wasted no time gathering the unit and every vehicle we could muster, then gave the order to move toward the village. The instructions were clear and strict: we were not to fire at the enemy unless they fired at us first. As we approached the outskirts of town, we saw terrified villagers running for their lives, desperate for any hope of safety.

Every second felt critical—turning back could mean life or death for these families. I was behind the wheel of a two-and-a-half-ton truck, a massive vehicle armed with a mounted fifty-caliber machine gun. We packed as many people as possible into the truck, filling every available space. The sense of urgency was overwhelming; the risks were real for both my team and the civilians. As soon as we were loaded, we sped away, hoping to deliver them to safety. But our escape was abruptly halted by the military police, known as MPs, who are responsible for enforcing regulations and maintaining order within the armed forces.

Riding with me was my platoon daddy—a term we used for the senior non-commissioned officer, the leader of our platoon and the one we all relied on for experience and guidance. We were at the head of the convoy and had managed to secure some buses to help evacuate even more villagers who were following our lead. But when we reached the MPs blocking the road, we were ordered to stop and unload everyone from our vehicles.

According to the United Nations' directives, we were forbidden from intervening in the crisis unfolding before us. The cease-fire was in effect, and we were told to stand down. I felt a deep frustration and helplessness wash over me—the rules demanded we stand by, but the Iraqi soldiers terrorizing the village clearly were not bound by the same restrictions. The gravity of the situation weighed heavily on me; every moment lost put innocent lives at greater risk, and I couldn't shake the sense that we were betraying the trust of those we had tried so desperately to help.

This made no sense to me; we had been deployed to protect civilians in a village that was being targeted by Iraqi soldiers—men we had previously disarmed and released after the cease-fire, in accordance with orders. Our mission up to that point had been to neutralize hostile forces and ensure the safety of innocent lives, so being told to stand down and allow these people to be slaughtered felt like a complete contradiction of our purpose.

We pleaded with the military police, insisting that if we didn't intervene, the villagers would almost certainly die, but our argument was overruled by United Nations directives. The MPs explained that, due to ongoing political negotiations and the strict terms of the cease-fire, we were forbidden from taking any further action, and any attempt to do so would result in our arrest.

I understand that the MPs were simply following orders, and I don't hold anything against them personally; they were in a difficult position as well. At the same time, the situation underscored the painful reality of war, where political decisions can sometimes clash with the immediate moral imperative to help those in danger. While I can see the complexity the UN faced in trying to maintain a fragile peace, I can't help but feel a deep sense of frustration and disappointment toward their decision in this case.

The most difficult thing I have ever had to do was to tell these people I could not help them. There are many things that I have trouble remembering about that time so many years ago, but what I remember vividly and relive every day is a father standing there with his young son who was about the same age of my nephew back home, pleading with me to help them. He spoke a little English, and his last words to me were "If you don't help us, my little boy is going to die."

We had to turn our back on these people and walk away. It's been over thirty years and this scene plays over in my head on a regular basis. This event has created a life full of what-ifs. What if I had just ignored the orders and saved them anyway? I would've been arrested, and they would have been left to die anyway. It still doesn't help. This is a moment in time that I will always regret and have had to just learn to live with it. But thankfully God understands these moments in our lives better than anyone, and if we allow him to, he will help us to cope and get through it.

After my service, I prayed to serve others with a Bible instead of a rifle, hoping to help people, especially children. Seventeen years later, that prayer was answered, bringing me peace and understanding.

I sat staring at this scripture about orphans and widows, trying to figure out what I was supposed to do with it. I knew God was trying to show me something, but I didn't know what. So I did the only thing that I knew to do: pray. The sense of uncertainty left me feeling both anxious and expectant, as if something significant was about to unfold but I had no idea what form it would take. While I was seeking guidance on one side of the world, across the globe, Syam was lifting up his own requests, pouring out his heart to God for help with the orphans in his care. Little did I know that as my prayers were going up to the Father, they were meeting with the prayers of a young pastor in India named Syam. Realizing that our prayers were intersecting in ways I could never have orchestrated myself filled me with awe and deepened my faith, reminding me just how powerfully God weaves lives together in the most unexpected ways. It truly was a perfect fit in the prayer room of grace.

I had created this website for what was to be our evangelistic ministry, where people could contact us through email and schedule us to come to their church. However, those were not the emails I began to receive. Instead, messages started pouring in from other countries, mostly from people seeking help. It quickly became clear that this was a common practice—foreigners reaching out to what they thought were rich Americans. Some requests were genuine, but many turned out to be scams. Even so, I would read through most of them, trying to figure out what God's will was amid all the noise and uncertainty. And then, one email stood out from all the rest, catching my attention in a way none of the others had. The experience left me both curious and reflective, wondering what God was trying to show me through it all.

I didn't responded to very many of the emails. The ones I did respond to was with your basic "I'll be praying for you." But when I read the email from Pastor Syam, it really touched my heart and the Holy Spirit was nudging me to respond. I emailed him back, and we instantly became good friends. He shared his testimony with me of how he had become a Christian and God called him into ministry to help care for the many orphans on the street.

He talked about how the kids would approach him on the street and God would tell him to take them in, even though he had his own family to care for and didn't have much room. Parents would abandon their kids on his doorstep because they just couldn't provide for them, and Syam had no choice but to take them in. He didn't understand why God was putting these children in his care when he didn't have the room or the ability to feed them.

When I met him, he was up to about fifteen orphans. Our relationship grew, and thanks to current technology, we were able to meet him and the children through video for the first time. The moment I saw those children, they stole my heart. And then the scripture that had me baffled about the orphans and widows became clear to me.

I didn't know what we would be able to do for them, but I knew we had to do something, so my wife and I began helping them with food. For the first several months, we met with them every week through video and made sure they had food.

Syam asked me to come to India and visit them in person so I began praying about going to India. My wife and I both worked, but we really didn't have any extra money lying around to fly to India, so I prayed that if God wanted me to go, he would have to provide for it. If it's his will, it's his bill.

It wasn't long after that when I received a check from a lady in our church who said God had told her to give me some money. It just so happened it was the amount I needed for a round-trip ticket to India. I knew then that I was going to India.

Once the word got out that I was going to India, others began donating to the mission, covering all expenses for the trip. Some would begin to tell me about the persecution Christians were facing there and I would cut them off. "Don't want to hear about it" was my response. I checked the map of where I was going but refused to look for any information about Christians being persecuted there.

Some might consider this to be careless, but I didn't want to come across anything that would cause me to second-guess what I knew was God's will. I learned some things about their culture and how they lived because I didn't want to go over and offend anyone that I might meet. I basically got on a plane and flew to a country that I had little knowledge of, without knowing what I was going into.

I thought Iraq and Saudi Arabia were a culture shock. They have nothing on India. The first thing that blew me over was the smell—a smell that remains in your nostrils for many days after. Not only was the smell strong, but I had never seen so many people in one place in my entire life. My first thought when I stepped out of that airport was Dear God, what have you gotten me into? And as if the smell and population weren't bad enough, there was about a ten-hour car ride that was more frightening than any plane I had ever jumped out of. They had one speed-fast, and then there's the constant horn honking that goes on day and night. I had never felt so out of place in my life, but I knew I was supposed to be there.

We were traveling to a part of India that not many Americans traveled to; it wasn't on the popular destination travel list, you could say.

Our hotel was next door to one of the many temples, and everywhere you looked, there were carved images of false gods that they worshipped regularly. I would sit outside on our balcony in the morning and read my Bible, and the pages came to life. I began understanding Paul's writings in ways I never had before.

I went to meet the children for the first time, and that was all it took for me. This was suddenly the most beautiful place on earth, and Link to Hope Ministries was born.

A New Home

Syam was doing all he could to care for these children, but his resources were painfully limited. They were crowded into a filthy, rat-infested two-room apartment. Just outside the front door sat a large pile of garbage, producing a stench unlike anything I had ever experienced. In many parts of the city, trash was dumped in heaps along the streets or outskirts and then set on fire. Even basic sanitation was almost nonexistent. If someone needed to use the restroom, they often simply relieved themselves in the drainage ditch beside the road—unless a sign happened to declare it a "No Urine Zone."

I remember when my first day with the children came to an end and we started back to our hotel. I turned and looked at their home—and I use that word loosely. In that moment, God spoke clearly to my heart: "I am going to build them a new home." The impression was so strong, and I believed it so fully, that I immediately said to Syam, "Syam, God is going to build you a new home." Without hesitation, he replied, "Let's look for some land."

I had not been a licensed minister for very long, and I had never preached with an interpreter before, but every calling has its first step. For several days, we preached a revival, and many people were saved and healed. It was an incredible experience—one that stretched me far beyond my comfort zone. On that same trip, I baptized people for the first time in the Indian Ocean. With the waves crashing against us, it was challenging, but it was also deeply meaningful.

Yet for me, nothing compared to the time I spent with those children. I did not understand then that God was doing a healing work inside me, but now I can see it.

Before it was time for us to leave, Syam found a piece of land for us to consider. It was a small plot, but at that time it seemed to be the only available place where we could build. We would not have been able to build anything very large, but anything would have been better than the conditions they were living in. We reached an agreement with the landowner and then returned home with the challenge of raising the money to buy it.

What we did not know was that God had something far greater in mind. He often does.

By the time I arrived back in America, the landowner had sold the property to someone else right out from under us. It was deeply disappointing and difficult to understand. I had been so sure that this was God's will, and I remember thinking, God, what happened? But Scripture reminds us that His ways are higher than ours. In our humanity, we often set goals at a level we think we can achieve, while God is calling us to believe for something only He can accomplish. So, we kept praying, trusting God to provide the land where their new home would eventually stand.

Not long after that, I received a message from Syam saying that a farmer was offering to sell us a piece of land outside Bapatla. The location was better, the property was much larger, and it would allow us to build a bigger facility in a safer area for the children.

After praying, we felt the best way to move forward was one step at a time. First, we would buy the land. Then, as funds came in, we would begin construction. It became a journey of faith and patience. In every season, God provided exactly what was needed for that appointed time. We never seemed to have more than enough, but we always had what we needed—and often felt nothing short of miraculous.

When enough money had come in, we purchased the property and started drawing up plans for the new facility. It did not take long to realize that Syam's vision for the orphanage was much larger than what we had originally discussed. The plans were far more ambitious than I had expected. Still, if this was truly God's direction, then He would surely make a way. And He did.

Through the generosity of local churches and kindhearted supporters, we raised enough money to begin the foundation. Everything seemed to be progressing well. Then, without warning, it all stopped. The money stopped coming in, and construction was put on hold. By then, the site had been prepared and the foundation had already been poured before everything came to a sudden halt. I did not yet know what was wrong, but deep down I sensed that something was off.

We decided to make another trip to visit the children and check on the construction. I had not been back since the land was purchased and work had begun, so I was eager to see the progress for myself.

Sometime before we bought the property, I had a dream about the orphanage. In that dream, we approached the facility from the road and saw a large iron gate with a pink wall across the front. Beside the orphanage, on the neighboring property, was another building that looked like a church.

When I woke up, I believed God was showing me what the orphanage would one day look like. What I did not understand then was that the dream was not a glimpse of the future, but confirmation.

The first time we approached the construction site, I was stunned. There stood the large iron gate exactly as I had seen it in my dream. It was not on our property, but on the neighboring land—the same property that would later be offered to us. And near that gate stood an old church that had been there for years. In that moment, I realized God had not shown me what was going to be there. He had shown me what was already there, as a confirmation that this was the place He had chosen.

It was thrilling to see the progress that had been made, but it was obvious that something was wrong. We just did not know what it was at first. However, the more time we spent walking the site and talking with Syam and the head engineer, the more the problem came into focus. This was not merely a practical issue. It was a spiritual one.

To begin with, the man overseeing the project was showing up late, and when he did arrive, he was often intoxicated. Beyond that, many of the construction workers were Hindu and did not want a Christian ministry to succeed in that place. They had been speaking curses over the new facility in an effort to stop the work. The flow of finances had dried up because God was not going to release more provision for the project until this issue was confronted. We did not learn the full story until after we returned home, but God was already preparing to do another miracle.

While we were there, we gathered at the construction site and prayed against the enemy's attack on the ministry. We did not yet know all the ways Satan was working, but we knew enough to stand in prayer. The Holy Spirit led us in how to pray. We remained for a couple more nights, preached, baptized several more converts, and then made our way home.

Not long after we returned home, the money started coming in again, and construction was able to move forward. Later, Syam told us about the miracle that had taken place after we had prayed and departed. The man overseeing the construction—the same man who had been showing up drunk and who had been a deeply committed Hindu—gave his life to Christ.

We later spoke with him on Skype, and he openly told us about the things he had done and the hatred he once had toward Christians. But something changed when we came and prayed over the construction site. He said he felt something real. He saw our devotion to God and became convinced that our God was alive, real, and listening to our prayers. In that moment, he surrendered his life to Christ. Today, he is a member of our Link to Hope board, part of our church there, and doing wonderfully.

From that point forward, God began moving on the hearts of people in our small community to support the mission in extraordinary ways. One dear friend and mentor, who was selling their house in town to move to the country, placed the keys in our hands and told us to sell it for whatever we could and use the money to help build the orphanage.

Checks began arriving from people I never would have expected, often in astonishing amounts. Still, it was never an overflow. It was always exactly what was needed for that particular season. God designed it that way so we would continue to rely on Him and trust His perfect timing. I have long believed that if someone is making a comfortable living from a nonprofit, then it has stopped being a nonprofit. It has become a business and ought to be presented as one.

Since the completion of the new orphanage, we have watched two of our young ladies get married and begin families of their own. We have also been able to provide the children with opportunities to attend college and continue their education, giving them hope for the future as they step into adulthood. Most importantly, they are being taught by wonderful teachers who are raising them in righteousness and teaching them how to pray. These children know what God has done for them, and they understand the hope and new life He has placed before them.

This mission has now continued for ten years. We currently care for up to twenty-five children and four widows, and we are also working to help people in the surrounding area who are suffering from AIDS. But for me, these past ten years have also been marked by healing and restoration. The more time I spend with these children, serving as their link to hope, the less I live in the guilt of the children I could not save.

Thank You, Jesus, for bringing these children into my life and for healing my heart. I love You.

Chapter 8: The Fall

I'm not sure what you may be thinking as you read this book.

Over the years, I have had people call me a prayer warrior, a man of God, and even a man after God's own heart. But I need you to understand something clearly: every example I have shared in this book about God speaking to me, about spiritual battles, and about the founding of Link to Hope Ministries in India came after a devastating fall from grace that left me in the darkest pit of my life, facing the choice between life and death.

Because of that, I cannot and will not take credit for any good that has come from my life. God alone deserves that glory. It is only by His mercy that I am still here, still breathing, and still able to serve Him at all. Every day I thank Him for giving me another chance to live the right way. To God be all the glory.

This is the chapter I most wanted to avoid writing. But I cannot leave it out.

If I did, this book would tell only part of the story. And without this part, you cannot fully understand redemption, the power of prayer, or the depth of God's forgiveness. This was the season when I discovered who I really was apart from God—and what I was capable of becoming when I chose the flesh over obedience. It was not pretty. And I pray that as my family and friends read these pages, they will see not only my failure, but the mercy of God that met me there.

One of the great blessings of my life is that I was raised by parents who loved God and did everything they knew to raise me in the ways of righteousness. I was taught the value of prayer, the importance of God's Word, and the difference between right and wrong. I do not take that lightly. I know many people never receive that kind of foundation, and I am grateful that I did.

Proverbs 22:6 reminds us to train up a child in the way he should go, and when he is old, he will not depart from it. I count myself blessed to have had parents who did everything they knew to raise me in righteousness. Yet as many of us have seen, even faithful parents can watch a child turn away from that foundation and pursue the desires of the flesh.

I believe one vital part of spiritual training is too often neglected, and because of that, many people eventually drift from the faith they once professed: they never truly discover God for themselves.

Many of us grow up in church learning how to pray, why we should read the Bible, and how to recognize the difference between right and wrong. But knowing those things is not the same as personally knowing God. When we are young, we often lean on the faith of our parents, and for a time, that may seem enough. But as we get older and the pull of the world grows stronger, if we have not come to know God for ourselves, we become vulnerable to sin and can quickly find ourselves in bondage to it.

Like a lot of teenagers raised in church, I had my spiritual highs followed by nights of compromise. One week I would come home from church camp feeling fully surrendered to God, convinced nothing could pull me away, and the next week I would be chasing the pleasures of the world. Not every teenager follows that path, and I have great respect for those who stayed faithful through it all. But as a young man who had not yet truly grasped what it meant to know God for myself, I lived on that revolving door between faith and sin. I am deeply grateful that God sees not only who we are, but who we can become.

By the time I got married, my wife and I were faithful in church, and I believed I had developed a real relationship with God—or at least something close to it. When I entered the military, I went to basic training in Georgia, where I stayed committed to reading my Bible and holding on to my faith. After that, we were stationed at Fort Bragg, North Carolina. I continued trying to live according to what I had been taught, but it was becoming more difficult. As time went on and I spent more of my life away from home, I gradually slipped into what many would consider the typical soldier's lifestyle. We never found a church where we could get firmly planted, and that matters more than many people realize. Without that foundation, I began drifting farther away.

About a year into my time with the 82nd Airborne Division, I was spending my nights club hopping with the guys and drinking until I passed out in the barracks, while my wife sat home alone. Looking back, I know I was being a real jerk. One night I stumbled home drunk and got a serious warning from my wife: "If you ever come home like this again, I'm going back to Oklahoma." That got my attention. The last thing I wanted was to lose her, so I cleaned up my act for a while. I still had my slipups, but I kept them hidden. After all, what happened in the barracks stayed in the barracks.

Then came Operation Desert Shield/Storm, and suddenly I decided I probably needed God after all. So, in my own way, I became a Christian again. Funny how the reality of war can do that to a person. I had moments when I thought I was truly encountering God, but the truth is, I still did not understand what it meant to know Him personally.

After we were discharged from the Army, we moved back to Oklahoma in hopes of building a more normal life. We moved often, and I bounced from job to job, but we never really felt settled until we returned to our hometown. By then, we had two children—a boy and a girl born just over nine months apart. We had tried to have children for the first five years of our marriage, but apparently it just was not time yet. Then once the first baby arrived, it seemed like all I had to do was look at my wife the wrong way and she would get pregnant.

Our first child, Gehrig, arrived about six weeks early, and he has been in a hurry ever since. I was preparing to take my EMT (Emergency Medical Technician) test in Oklahoma City when I received a call that my wife was being flown there because she had gone into labor early. I was told I would not be allowed to reschedule the test, so I had no choice but to take it right then. I ran in, grabbed the exam, and completed it as fast as I could. I failed every section except the one on pregnancy and labor. Go figure.

After that, I rushed to the hospital, where our son was born. He spent some time in the ICU, and in order to stay near him, I took a job in Oklahoma City. We lived there for several years before eventually moving back to our hometown of Seiling. Then, just nine months and ten days later, Ashley was born. It felt like we had twins.

Now, a warning: this is where my shallowness begins to show.

After the children were born, my wife gained weight and had a hard time losing it. Childbirth changes a woman's body, and instead of responding with maturity and grace, I let my selfishness shape the way I viewed her. In my shallow mind, she no longer looked like the young blonde woman I had married. I am not proud to say that, but I am committed to being honest. As her appearance changed, the intimacy in our marriage slowly began to fade.

That became an excuse—one I allowed myself to believe—that would later help justify one of the worst sins of my life. The truth is, whether you are a man or a woman, the enemy knows how to spot those vulnerable places in a marriage, and he knows exactly how to exploit them.

Instead of sitting down and confronting our problems, we dealt with them the way we dealt with most things—we buried them and hoped they would go away. Maybe neither of us knew how to talk about something so personal, or maybe we were simply too embarrassed to try. Whatever the reason, that silence became a costly mistake for us both.

The enemy has a way of noticing the empty spaces in our lives, and he is always ready to fill them with fleshly desires when godly ones are missing. At the time, I still thought of myself as some kind of Christian. In a way, I was—but I did not truly understand what it meant to know God. That misunderstanding became part of my downfall.

One morning, on my way to work, I stopped for breakfast and met a young woman there. She was attractive, bold, and made her interest in me obvious from the beginning. She began showering me with attention, and I was hungry for it. The attention I no longer felt at home was now coming from someone else, and instead of rejecting it, I began to enjoy it. Before long, I was going to that restaurant regularly just to see her.

It was not the food that kept drawing me back. It was the feeling of being wanted. She pursued me relentlessly, and eventually we began meeting in secret. Before I fully grasped what I had become, I was involved in a relationship with another woman—one who knew exactly how to make lust feel like love. She knew I was married and did not care. What made it even more dangerous was that my feelings for her began to feel real. My mind had grown so distorted that I convinced myself my marriage had been a mistake and that this woman was somehow my true soulmate.

The affair went on for a while, and with each passing day I drifted farther from my family, farther from God, and deeper into darkness. I stopped going to church entirely. I could not bring myself to walk through those doors, because church had become a painful reminder of everything I had surrendered. By then, I had become a terrible husband, an absent father, and an adulterer.

Before long, I sank into a deep depression. It felt as though I were trapped alone in a vast, black hole, staring down a decision that would change everything: Do I stay, or do I go? My mistress wanted me to leave my family and be with her, and part of me wanted that too. But another part of me still wanted to save my marriage. As the pressure built, that question slowly turned into something even darker: Do I live, or do I die? That is how low I had fallen. When a person begins to contemplate suicide, they have entered a place of profound darkness.

I became a shell of the man I was supposed to be. I sat alone in the dark, pulling away from everyone, wanting nothing to do with anyone. Inside, I was shutting down. I felt as though I could not have what I wanted, and I no longer wanted what I had. The people around me noticed the change, but I refused to talk about it. In my mind, my life was shattered and no longer worth living.

Then two very important things happened.

I was sitting in my recliner, swallowed by the darkness I had fallen into, when an unusual thought came to me. It was a Wednesday night, and I had not been to church in quite a while. Yet out of nowhere, I found myself thinking, What if someone from the church comes by to check on me? That was the last thing I wanted.

By then, I had become so bitter towards the church that I had already made up my mind: if anyone came to my house, I was going to tell them to leave. I did not want anyone from church in my home, and I certainly did not want to talk to them—except for one man. There was one man in that church I respected too much to treat that way. Maybe it was because he had walked through some hard things himself. I remember thinking, if someone from the church shows up, I'm sending them away—unless it's him.

Sure enough, after church ended, there was a knock at the door—just as I had imagined. And, of course, it was the one person I could not turn away. I let him in. He sat down, talked with me, and read Scripture from his Bible. To be honest, I do not remember a single word he said. The only thing I could hear in that moment was this: God knew. God knew exactly who to send, and in that simple act, He was reminding me that He was still there.

The words themselves were not nearly as important as the act of obedience that brought him to my door. After our brief visit, he left, and I remained there in the dark, deep in thought. Wondering if God could still love me. Wondering if He could still want me. Wondering if my marriage could still be saved.

His visit helped prepare the ground and plant the seed for the next phase of what God was doing in my life. Not long after, my mom came over to the house and decided to stay. I was still sitting alone in the dark, hardly speaking to anyone, feeling as though I were hanging by a thread and dangerously close to letting go.

Like so many God-fearing mothers, my mom recognized that Satan was attacking my family. From the other room, I could hear her praying in the Spirit. I knew exactly what she was doing. She was going to war on my behalf, standing against the enemy, and she had no intention of backing down. I truly think the devil fears a praying mother or grandmother more than almost anything else on earth.

Those two acts of faith became lifelines for me in that season: Danny's obedience to God and my mother's prayers. I began to wonder if God really still cared about me. I began to wonder if He could actually forgive me. And the more I thought about it, the more it felt as though the Son—pun intended—was beginning to shine through the windows of the dark house I had been living in.

I knew then that a decision had to be made, and it had to be made now. The wrong choice would eventually lead to death. The right choice had painful and unknown consequences. One path was better than the other, but neither would be easy.

The first step I had to take was the hardest one of all: I had to tell my wife. There was no way around it.

Part of me thought that once I told her, she would make the decision for me. I knew how seriously God viewed divorce, but I also knew how seriously He viewed adultery. Jesus made that plain. He said that divorce was not God's design, except in the case of adultery (Matthew 19:9 NIV). Then He raised the standard even further by saying that even looking at someone lustfully is adultery in the heart (Matthew 5:28 NIV). Whether people want to admit it or not, pornography falls into that same category. So to me, this was no longer just my decision. It was hers too. I had no idea how she would respond, and what happened next caught me completely off guard.

I told her I needed to talk, and we sat together on the edge of our bed. Then I confessed that there was another woman in my life, that I was developing feelings for her, and that I did not know what to do. My wife began to cry. Then she knelt at my feet, looked up at me through her tears, and said, "It's your decision."

I was stunned. She was willing to forgive me, but she was also willing to let me go if that was what I chose. In that moment, I came face to face with the true meaning of love. We sat there together, both of us weeping under the weight of what stood before us. Her response broke something in me. Overwhelmed by her love, I chose to end the affair and fight for my marriage.

But it was not enough to ask my wife for forgiveness. I knew I had to go before God. So I prayed the best prayer I could manage, burdened with guilt and desperate for mercy. But I felt nothing. No peace. No comfort. Just emptiness. It was as if I were praying to a wall. Heaven felt silent.

I was determined not only to save my marriage, but to somehow win God back as well—or at least that is how I understood it at the time. I went back to reading my Bible, praying faithfully, and attending church, yet inside I felt nothing. It was like wandering in a desert, searching for water that never seemed to come. That season lasted for about three years. Then one day, as I knelt at the altar to pray, God finally spoke. I heard Him so clearly in my heart: "It's been long enough." In that moment, I felt His arms wrap around me in a way I had never known before, and all the pain and sorrow seemed to wash away in His presence.

That was when I finally understood.

God lifted me out of the darkness and into His light and set me on the road to redemption. Even so, the journey of restoring our marriage and rebuilding my wife's trust was long and painful. It took years, and in many ways, I am still tending to the places where trust was broken. Yet in the middle of that healing process, God gave us a precious gift in our youngest daughter, Brienna, who helped bring restoration to our family and draw us closer together.

The healing came, but the scars remained. Scars are the lasting evidence of wounds caused by the choices we make, whether sinful or sorrowful. Some wounds cut so deeply that their pain lingers for years. I still ache over the pain I caused my wife, and I pray every day that she will continue to love me. I also carry the guilt of that affair in more ways than I can express. The young woman I once believed I loved eventually took her own life, and I do not know whether the guilt of feeling responsible for her death will ever fully fade.

My wife never asked for the details of the affair—not who it was with or everything that happened. She simply took me back and forgave me. I know it was far more painful and complicated than those words can express, and I am sure the struggle did not end there. But she was willing to let God do what only He can do: redeem what has been broken and bring healing where there has been deep hurt. I will be forever grateful that she gave me a chance at redemption.

We have never shared this with our family, not even with our children. In fact, most of them will not know until they read these pages. My prayer is that they will respond with the same grace my wife showed me and the same mercy God has shown me, and that they will not think too harshly of me. We told only one other couple in our church, because they played a vital role in helping us move forward and, in many ways, saving my life. If not for that man, my mother's prayers, and my children, only God knows where I might have ended up. When it came down to the final choice, I could not bring myself to do that to my children. I could only hope that one day, when they learned what their father had done, they would find it in their hearts to forgive me.

My wife and I have kept this hidden for many years, but deep down I knew it would eventually need to be told. I just never imagined it would be printed in a book for the whole world to see. I am certain there will be people who judge me harshly. Some may lose respect for me. Some friends or family members may even distance themselves. But I had to tell it, because somewhere there is a man or woman—a potential hero of faith—who needs to know that God can redeem them no matter who they are or what they have done. God can heal a broken home. He can restore meaning to a life that feels hopeless. Some of His greatest miracles are worked through people who have been humbled by the wreckage of their own most devastating choices.

Over time, I began to see my wife for who she truly is: a hero of faith. She may not look exactly like the young woman I married, but she became the woman I desperately needed. She revealed that heroic faith when she chose to forgive me and love me in spite of who I had become and what I had done. Anyone who knows my wife would likely describe her as kind, caring, and deeply loving. But what many do not fully see is her strength, or all that she has endured. Most people know about the way she cared for our daughter during her battle with cancer, but almost no one knows the battles she fought behind closed doors to save our family. That is why I say the hero of faith in this book is not me, but my wife. I did not just encounter a hero of faith for this generation, I married her.

Although this book is filled with my own story of coming to know God in a deeply personal way, that story would have unfolded very differently had she not chosen to forgive me and continue loving me.

Forgiveness and love are two of the defining marks of a true hero of faith, and I can only hope and pray that one day I will grow into that same depth of faith myself.

Because she gave me another chance, I was able to come to know God in the way He had always intended. For years, I did not understand that. God does not want a shallow relationship built on habit, tradition, or man-made religious systems. He wants something personal, intimate, and fully surrendered. If we truly want to experience Him in the way Scripture describes, then we must be willing to lay everything down before Him. He must become the highest priority in our lives. We must seek Him with all our heart, soul, and mind, and we must obey His Word. The discovery of who God truly is—and how to walk in personal relationship with Him—is found in Scripture. If we neglect His Word, we should not expect to know Him deeply.

I have heard people teach that the Christian life is not about rules and regulations, and that salvation cannot be gained through human effort. That much is true. Salvation is free. It cannot be earned, purchased, or achieved by works. But while salvation is freely given, holiness is not something that happens without response on our part. Holiness requires surrender. It requires obedience. It requires effort.

God does call His people to live by certain standards. Righteousness begins with faith in Christ as the risen Savior, but genuine faith reveals itself through obedience to His Word. We cannot be righteous without Jesus, and we cannot claim to know Jesus while willfully rejecting His commands. Colossians 3 makes this clear in its teaching on holy living, and the rest of the New Testament is filled with instruction for how a believer ought to live. Salvation is always free, but holiness is pursued when we deny ourselves, take up our cross, and follow Him. In denying ourselves and obeying His Word, we come to know Him more fully. And in that process, we also learn that He lovingly disciplines His children when they sin.

There is a difference between unintentional sin and intentional sin. When we knowingly choose rebellion, God disciplines us—not because He delights in punishment, but because He loves us too much to leave us there. It is much like the parent who says, "As long as you live under my roof, you will follow my rules." The same principle applies in the family of God. If we are going to be His children, then we must live in a way that honors Him, pleases Him, and helps build His kingdom rather than undermine it.

Few things damage the kingdom more than a person who claims to belong to God while consistently living in opposition to His Word. That is hypocrisy. And hypocrisy will destroy your witness faster than almost anything else. Once that credibility is lost, it can be very difficult to recover.

The important thing to remember is that God has given us everything we need to live a holy and righteous life (2 Peter 1:3 NIV). He does not simply offer us a few principles and then send us into the world to figure it out on our own. As we grow in intimate relationship with Him, we begin to realize that we are no longer called to live according to the flesh, which brings bondage, but according to the Spirit, who brings freedom. It is through the Spirit that we come to understand His will and are empowered to do the works this world needs to see to know that God is real.

Our works do not save us, but faith without works is dead. Even though holy living requires effort on our part, that effort is ultimately an expression of faith—trusting that God can use our lives to accomplish His perfect will. The works we do are not produced by human strength alone, but through His power, His wisdom, and His understanding working in us. His ways are far above ours, and we may never fully understand them in this life. But if we understood everything, there would be no need for faith.

Faith is expressed not only through holy living, but also through the works we do in God's name. These works are the acts of obedience and love that reflect His heart to the world. They include giving to those in need, praying for the sick, preaching, teaching, and serving in worship. They are the result of taking the gifts and abilities God placed within us and using them to share the gospel of Jesus Christ so that others may come to know Him.

Scripture calls us to strive for holiness (Hebrews 12:14 NIV). To strive means to make every effort— to pursue something with determination because it matters deeply to us. A righteous and holy life must become something we desire above all else. We will not walk in it casually. It is something we must pursue intentionally, while remembering that we do not pursue it in our own strength. As we seek holiness, God supplies the strength, discipline, and perseverance required to walk it out. To strive for perfection is to become fully focused on what it takes to attain it, and in this case, that means keeping our eyes fixed on Jesus Christ, the author and finisher of our faith.

All of us will make mistakes in our journey to know God, but we must be especially wary of intentional sin. Those choices, when left unrepented of, lead toward death. When I look back on my own descent into darkness, I now see it as a painful but powerful lesson. As devastating as it was, it taught me how Satan watches for weakness and seizes every opportunity to bring destruction. But it also taught me that he only gains that ground when we are not walking closely with God. If we neglect the Word of God and abandon our prayer life, we become only a weak imitation of true Christianity, and the enemy will exploit that weakness every time.

Sin is always waiting at the door, looking for an opening to step in and wreak havoc in the life of anyone pursuing God. Stay close to Him, and He will remain near to you. When fleshly desires rise up and temptation tries to plant the seed of sin that leads to death, you can overcome through Christ, because in Him we are more than conquerors.

For years, I carried the guilt of my daughter's cancer. In my mind, that terrible disease was connected to the choices I had made. I felt as though she was suffering because of my sin, and that was a heavy burden to bear. Even now, I cannot say that I fully understand it all. But this much I do know: God has an extraordinary way of taking our failures, our sins, and our deepest regrets and using them for good. He can take what is broken and painful and somehow turn it into something that brings Him glory—if we are willing to surrender it to Him.

As for me, I do not consider myself to have attained the title of "hero of faith." But I pursue it daily. I want to be the person God can count on—the one willing to stand in the gap so that judgment might be withheld from a people because one faithful servant was still willing to obey. I want to be the one who stands for truth when no one else will. I want to love the people others have given up on. I want to preach the gospel, even if doing so costs me everything.

I want to be someone God can always trust to care for the poor, the weak, and the overlooked.

The battle lines between good and evil have been drawn, and this world is being divided by truth and falsehood, righteousness and rebellion. Evil is praised, while righteousness is often mocked and condemned. God is not looking for a powerless, compromised Christianity, nor for people who profess His name while denying His Word through hypocrisy. He is looking for true disciples of Jesus Christ—people who will deny the flesh, reject the spirit of this age, and rise up as genuine heroes of faith.

Chapter 9: The End-Time War

The battle of Armageddon draws a great deal of attention whenever the subject of the last days comes up. It will be the mother of all wars and a glorious day for those who have remained faithful to the truth. But even now, we are caught in a battle that may be the most important war of our generation. It is not the physical conflicts we have faced in the fight against terrorism, nor the wars fought in places like Afghanistan and Iraq.

Though it is not a physical war in the way Armageddon will be, it is every bit as real and far more present than many realize. It is vital that we understand it and take it seriously. The greatest war of our time is spiritual, and it cannot be won by human strength or fleshly effort. It can only be won in the spiritual realm by true heroes of faith.

This war is not ultimately about politics, celebrities, or cultural figures. It is not merely about socialism or conservatism. At its deepest level, it is still the age-old conflict between God and Satan, between righteousness and rebellion, between good and evil. Satan has already rallied his forces, and the cultural battles we see around us are simply weapons being used in an attempt to gain ground in a war whose final outcome has already been settled.

There was a time when evil worked more quietly, hiding in the shadows. But in recent years, that has changed. The gloves have come off. Evil is no longer simply tolerated; it is openly celebrated, promoted, and even applauded in ways we have not seen before. Looking back to the 1960s, it becomes clear that there was more taking place than a military draft for Vietnam. In another sense, there was also a spiritual recruitment underway for the battle we are facing now. Many believed they were entering a new age of enlightenment, when in reality they were opening themselves to deception.

To widen that influence, the enemy used powerful tools—drugs and persuasive voices. Under the influence of substances like LSD and other drugs, the mind can become dangerously vulnerable, easily shaped by those who know how to manipulate it. In that condition, destructive ideas can be made to appear wise, liberating, or compassionate. And once enough hearts and minds have been influenced, those same ideas can continue spreading even without the drugs. At that point, all that is required is to convince the next generation that they are entitled to gain without sacrifice, receive without responsibility, and demand what belongs to others.

The enemy is not only after minds dulled by drugs. He is after the hearts and minds of the next generation, and he has worked to infiltrate places of influence, including our schools, with an agenda rooted in confusion and sexual immorality. The fact that drag queens are reading to kindergartners, and that children are being taught they can choose from many genders, ought to be a wake-up call to the church that we have been asleep for too long. While the enemy has advanced his agenda, too few heroes of faith have been willing to stand in the gap and resist it.

This battle is deeper than politics. It is not simply a war against socialism, liberalism, or conservatism. It is a spiritual war against Satan and the powers of darkness, and it is more visible and active now than ever before. It will not be won by polished programs or impressive church buildings. It will be won by true disciples of Jesus Christ. The church is where believers gather to worship, learn, encourage one another, and be equipped. But it is not the battlefield, and it must never become a social club.

Now is not the time for Christians to be passive, fearful, or weak. Now is the time for new heroes of faith to rise up and contend for truth and for the souls of men and women. Throughout the

Bible, we repeatedly see moments when God says, "Rise up and go." And many times, that command is followed by a miracle.

A powerful example of this is Philip and the Ethiopian official in Acts 8:26–40. God told Philip to rise up and go south to the road from Jerusalem to Gaza. There he encountered a man from Ethiopia reading the prophet Isaiah but unable to understand what he was reading. Philip joined him, explained the Scripture, and shared the good news of Jesus Christ. The man believed and was baptized. Then Philip was suddenly taken away and later found at Azotus, where he continued preaching the gospel. God sent Philip down that desert road for the sake of one man—an influential official in charge of the treasury of Candace, queen of the Ethiopians. Just imagine the impact that man may have had when he returned home carrying the truth of Christ back to Ethiopia.

Another powerful example is Ananias (Acts 9:10–19 NIV). God told him to "rise and go" to the house of Judas on Straight Street and ask for a man from Tarsus named Saul. Ananias hesitated because he had already heard of Saul's reputation as a persecutor of the church. But despite his concerns, he obeyed. He rose up and went. Saul, in turn, had also been told by Jesus to rise and go into the city, where he would be shown what to do and where his sight would be restored. In that moment of obedience, Saul was healed and ultimately transformed by the truth of Christ.

Saul had hated the church and committed terrible acts against Christians. He stood in approval of Stephen's execution and made it his mission to destroy the followers of Jesus. The hatred we see directed at the church today is not something new. It has existed from the very beginning.

So what makes the difference?

If you look carefully at those who responded when God said, "Rise up and go," you will see a common thread: they were true disciples of Jesus Christ. They were not Christians in name only, nor were they merely religious people going through motions. They followed the teachings of Christ, submitted themselves to God's will, denied their own desires, and gave themselves fully to the work they had been called to do. They followed Jesus wholeheartedly, and most were willing to die for that commitment.

That is where much of the church struggles today. There is too much sitting and waiting, and not enough rising and going. We have become comfortable, technologically advanced, and in many cases more concerned with pleasing the flesh than strengthening the spirit. Where are the miracles, signs, and wonders that are meant to follow true disciples? Can such disciples still be found in our time?

A true disciple is a hero of faith, and that is exactly what we need for the battles of these last days. The early disciples carried truth, faith, prayer, obedience, and the power of the Holy Spirit. Nothing about God's method has changed. Those are still the things required today. Yet far too often, they have been replaced by comfort, technology, and entertainment.

It will take heroes of faith like Philip and Ananias—men and women willing to rise up, go where God sends them, and speak the truth to those He places in their path. Many people who are now viewed as vile, broken, or beyond hope may be just one Damascus Road encounter away from salvation. As dark and disturbing as things in this country may seem, we cannot allow hatred to settle in our hearts. We can stand against deception. We can stand for the unborn. But we must not hate.

Jesus told us to pray for those who persecute us, not to retaliate against them. That is the response of a true disciple. It is not our place to write people off because of their words, their lifestyles, or their rebellion. God will judge in His perfect time. Our calling is to rise up and be witnesses to the truth of Jesus Christ before a lost world.

We are called to rise and go into our workplaces with the intention of reflecting Christ through both our conduct and our words. We are called to rise and go to the hurting, to help those in need, and to pray for the sick. We are called to rise up and carry the message of salvation to anyone, anywhere, at any time God directs us. As Jesus said, we are to "go and make disciples of all nations, baptizing them in the name of the Father and of the Son and of the Holy Spirit." The goal is not to produce imitation Christians, but true disciples.

True Repentance

Before we can ever become true disciples or heroes of faith, we must repent. We must turn from our old life and old ways with no desire to return to them. I see the lack of this all too often, and I know it well because I was once guilty of it myself. Many people profess faith in Jesus, are baptized, and then continue living in ways that dishonor the very name they claim.

A powerful example of this is Simon the Sorcerer in Acts. Before the gospel came to Samaria, Simon had captivated the people with his sorcery. They were amazed by him and considered him a man of great power. Simon himself encouraged that belief, presenting himself as someone important. For years the people followed him because he dazzled them. But when Philip arrived preaching the good news of Jesus Christ, many believed and were baptized—including Simon (Acts 8:9–25 NIV).

At first, that sounds like a wonderful testimony. A man so deeply caught up in deception appears to believe the gospel and respond in baptism. But as the story unfolds, it becomes clear that Simon's response was only external. When Peter and John came and began laying hands on the new believers so they could receive the Holy Spirit, Simon's true condition was revealed. Amazed by what he saw, he offered the apostles money in exchange for that power.

Peter rebuked him immediately. He told Simon that his heart was not right before God and that he had no part in this ministry because he thought the gift of God could be bought. Peter saw beyond the outward profession and exposed the inward reality: Simon was still full of bitterness and bound by sin. Even after believing and being baptized, his heart had not truly changed.

Terrified by Peter's words, Simon begged for prayer so that judgment would not come upon him.

Peter's response was direct: repent. Repent, and ask God to forgive the wickedness in your heart.

Simon believed the message and took the outward steps, but he had not come to a place of true surrender. He still wanted to hold on to his position, his image, and his sense of power. He was willing to believe, but not willing to humble himself completely before God. That same problem exists today. Many believe, many are baptized, and many even look the part, but their motives remain impure and their hearts remain unchanged. Without repentance, they become Christians in name only.

True conversion is marked by humility and repentance. It cannot be purchased, earned, inherited, or imitated. It is given freely to anyone—no matter who they are or what they have done—when they truly turn from sin and follow Christ.

I have heard many so-called Christians complain about older churches because they say all those churches preach are rules, regulations, and a long list of dos and don'ts. They insist that Christianity is not about rules and regulations. But the danger is that many have reacted so strongly against legalism that they have drifted into lawlessness, treating God's commandments as if they were optional or burdensome. In doing so, they fail to obey even the most basic teachings of Christ.

For many, the entire Christian experience has been reduced to a few popular Scriptures that fit their emotions and personal preferences. But our faith is not built on feelings, opinions, or cultural trends. It is built on the truth of what God has spoken—not just the parts we like, but the whole counsel of His Word. Scripture is clear: if we love Him, we will obey Him. It is not complicated, even if it is costly.

But if we are not studying the Word of God, how can we possibly know what He requires of us? Is our faith built only on a Sunday sermon or on whatever the latest charismatic preacher happens to say? We are commanded to test the spirits to discern what is true, and the only way to do that is by measuring everything against the Word of God.

Prisoners of War

A prisoner of war (POW) is a soldier who has been captured by the enemy, taken out of the fight, and placed under the enemy's control. He no longer has the freedom or ability to stand alongside his fellow soldiers in battle. Instead, he is bound and forced to live according to the enemy's rule.

In the spiritual battles of these last days, the enemy still takes prisoners. They may not sit behind bars in a literal cell, but they are no less captive. They are bound, hindered, and removed from the fight in ways that are often less visible but just as real. In this chapter, I want to address some of the most common forms of that captivity. If the previous chapters have shown anything, it should be clear that while I may not be an expert on this subject, I do know what it is like to be a prisoner in the war we are called to fight.

One of the most common ways the enemy takes people captive is through anxiety. Anxiety disorders seem to be increasing and have become especially common, even among believers. There is a reason for that, and it is not hard to see. Anxiety has become one of Satan's most effective weapons. It can grow so intense that a person loses the ability to function as they once did. Over the last five years, anxiety has likely been the greatest battle of my own life.

I can still remember being told that if you struggle with anxiety—or take medication for it—then your faith must be weak. The same verse is almost always quoted: Philippians 4:6 (NIV), the passage that tells us not to be anxious about anything. But there is more to that scripture than a surface reading allows, and it must be studied carefully to understand what it is truly saying. It does not mean a believer will never battle anxiety, nor does it promise that anxiety simply vanishes. What it does reveal is how we are to walk through it. The answer is found in prayer, petition, and thanksgiving.

When I look back, I can see that anxiety had probably been part of my life for years. Anytime I had to speak in front of people, I would become intensely nervous and fearful. I did not like large crowds then, and I still do not. Even now, I am particular about where I sit in public places. But it was not until five or six years ago, when I became a pastor and took on greater responsibility in ministry, that the anxiety truly began to overwhelm me.

The first time I experienced a full anxiety attack, I was convinced I was having a stroke. I ended up in the emergency room three separate times before we finally discovered that I was dealing with a severe anxiety disorder. That was a hard reality for me to accept. In my mind, I was a child of God, and I thought that meant He was supposed to simply take anxiety away.

Because of that thinking, I refused medication. To me, it felt like admitting weakness. So I tried to endure each attack as it came. But over time, preaching became harder and harder, and every

Sunday became a battle. I had always been the kind of preacher who depended entirely on the Holy Spirit, because on my own I was simply too nervous. Most of the time, I would remain anxious until I began preaching, and once the Spirit took over, I would be fine.

But eventually, even that started to change.

I prayed, fasted, and did everything I thought a faithful Christian was supposed to do in order to get free from anxiety, but instead of getting better, it only grew worse. And as if the anxiety were not enough, I also began to experience severe physical pain. The pain would strike in the back of my head with such intensity that I would nearly pass out. It felt like someone was jabbing an ice pick into the base of my skull. What made it even stranger was that it only seemed to happen when I was preaching or involved in some kind of spiritual warfare. It was unlike anything I had ever felt.

I went back to my doctor again. I underwent scans, tests, and evaluations, but every result came back the same: nothing was wrong. Yet the pain kept getting worse. It reached the point where I would have to stop mid-sermon and ask the congregation to pray for me so I could finish preaching. Eventually, it became so severe that I had to step outside for air just to keep from passing out. One Sunday morning, we moved the entire service outdoors and finished in the cool air, which seemed to help. My wife and I noticed that just before an attack, my ears would turn red and I would begin to sweat. Within a minute, the pain would hit.

By then, I had finally agreed to take the medication my doctor had recommended for anxiety. It seemed to help some, but inside I felt more and more like a prisoner.

In a small town, it is common for a pastor to work another job while serving the church, and that is exactly what I was doing. If anything, it made the struggle even harder. Between the anxiety and panic attacks, the demands of two jobs, and some painful family issues we were trying to work through, I eventually reached my breaking point.

It is hard for me to admit this, but I simply could not keep going.

One morning, my wife and I woke up and made one of the hardest decisions we had ever faced. We decided to leave—not just the church, but the entire state. We packed our things and moved to Missouri. We had always loved Branson. We had vacationed there often and had talked for years about living there someday. We just did not realize that day would come so quickly.

I knew I had to get away. I needed a long break from the weight of ministry. We were still connected to the orphanage and the work in India, but I was no longer preaching. Deep down, I felt that I needed at least a year away to sort through what was happening and find some measure of relief.

After living in Missouri for a few months and stepping away from preaching, I was asked to fill in for a pastor friend in Branson at one of the theaters. I hesitated at first, but I had been feeling better and convinced myself I was ready.

That Sunday morning, I was introduced and walked onto the stage. I got through about thirty seconds before the blinding pain struck. It was the most severe attack I had ever experienced. My wife immediately stepped in to take over while others helped me off the stage and outside for air. Usually the fresh air would bring some relief, but this time it was so intense that we had no choice but to go to the emergency room.

They ran test after test, but once again, nothing showed up. Then a day or two later, it happened again, and I found myself right back in the emergency room. More scans, more testing, and still no explanation. By that point, I could not even speak in a small meeting without triggering an attack. All I could do was sit quietly and keep silent.

After seeing several doctors in Missouri, I finally found one who was able to make sense of it all. I was diagnosed with agoraphobia, an anxiety disorder that can develop when repeated panic attacks go untreated—or at least that is how it was explained to me. Looking back, I can see that I had been foolish to minimize the panic attacks and assume they would eventually go away on their own instead of addressing them earlier. But at the time, I thought I was doing what a good Christian was supposed to do in the face of anxiety: pray, seek God, and trust that it would all disappear. But that is not always how God works.

God is our ever-present help in times of trouble. He promises to walk with us through every trial and tribulation and to carry us through them, but He does not always remove them. One of the clearest examples of this is found in Jesus before His arrest. Scripture says His sweat was like drops of blood as He prayed in deep anguish before the Father (Luke 22:42–44 NIV). He asked if it was possible for the cup before Him to be taken away. Just imagine the weight He was carrying in that moment, knowing exactly what lay ahead. Yet even though the Father could have removed that burden, He did not. Instead, He gave Jesus exactly what He needed to endure it. And He still does the same for us.

Anxiety disorders are an illness like many others, and they can be treated. When we get sick with a cold or the flu, we pray for healing. When serious illness comes to us or someone we love, we pray for the miracle we know God can do, while also seeking help and wisdom from doctors. Anxiety is no different. As I eventually learned, when it is left untreated, it can rob a person of the ability to function and even hinder them from doing the very things God has called them to do.

Looking back, I can now see how God led me through several stages, using each one to strengthen my faith and bring me to the place where I could finally receive the help and answers I needed. A doctor who is wise in medicine, yet also rooted in Scripture and prayer, is a true physician. My medications were adjusted and increased, and within a few weeks I began to improve. In time, I even returned to my hometown to preach for a dear friend. I was extremely nervous about stepping back into the pulpit, but considering how far I had fallen, it went remarkably well.

The right doctor and the right medication played an important part in my healing, but just as important—if not more so—was having a trusted person to talk with and pray alongside. God never intended for us to face these battles alone. Even Jesus had His disciples, though in His darkest hour they were asleep when He needed them most. In the same way, we have brothers and sisters in Christ to lean on when we are struggling.

So many Christians wrestle with anxiety and depression in silence because they are afraid it will make them appear spiritually weak. But like any other illness or struggle, it must be faced honestly and exposed for what it is: a weapon of the enemy. It is one of Satan's tools, designed to take us captive in this end-time battle and rob us of our ability to fight. As believers, we should make use of every provision God has made available to help us overcome whatever is keeping us from His will.

Living with an anxiety disorder has been one of the ways God has taught me, deepened my faith, and strengthened my perseverance. Some people are healed instantly from illness or disorder, while others walk a longer road. That does not mean their faith is weaker. It may simply mean that God has chosen a different path for them, one that carries its own lessons, growth, and purpose.

When we ask God to increase our faith, we should not be surprised if He allows trials and tribulations to become part of that journey. He brings us through difficulty, comforts us in the middle of it, and then uses what we have endured to help others facing similar battles. We are in a war, and I am determined to use every resource God has provided to remain in the fight and not become a prisoner of it.

Forgiveness

Forgiveness—or the refusal to give it—is another weapon the enemy uses to take Christians captive and turn them into prisoners in this war. I call it a weapon because it has the power either to destroy us or to set us free. Without forgiveness, there is no real hope and no lasting victory. If we will not forgive others, then we place ourselves outside the freedom of God's forgiveness. And without His forgiveness, we are eternally lost.

Forgiveness is one of the most difficult acts of obedience required of us as believers, yet it is absolutely necessary if we are going to walk in freedom. Our human nature wants to hold on to hurt, nurse old wounds, and strike back when we have been wronged. That is the way of the flesh. But it is not the way of God. When we become His, we are called to put the flesh to death and take on His nature instead. That does not happen overnight. It is formed through prayer, surrender, and a continual pursuit of God.

For me, the hardest person to forgive has been myself—and that may be the most dangerous kind of unforgiveness of all. If I cannot forgive myself, then I am binding my own hands while trying to fight a spiritual battle. It is like going to war with a rifle and no ammunition. I have counseled many people over the years, and my advice is always to forgive—especially themselves—so they can move forward. Many of them had fallen into sins similar to mine. Yet the very grace I urged them to receive was the one thing I could not seem to accept for myself. It was as though forgiveness was available for everyone else, but not for me.

That mindset kept me imprisoned for years. Guilt became a chain I dragged everywhere I went. But when God finally set me free, I was free indeed. It took prayer, faith, and discipline to reach the point where I could forgive myself and move beyond the things I had done, but every step was worth it. The enemy still tries to bring up my failures and remind me of my past, but I answer him quickly: it was all settled at the cross. And because Jesus overcame the world, I can walk in that victory too.

When we begin seriously seeking God and walking through the sanctification process, there often comes a point where we are required to go back and ask someone for forgiveness. That is one part of the journey I do not enjoy at all. If you are young and serious about following God, be careful about the choices you make, because there may come a day when you have to go back and make those things right—and that can be painfully humbling.

In my late teens, I made a couple of foolish and sinful decisions to steal. I knew right from wrong, and I believed in God, but I did not yet know Him in a real and personal way. Because of that, I was much more vulnerable to the quick desires of the flesh, and I gave in. One of those moments happened while I was dating the girl who would later become my wife. I stole money from her father, who is now my father-in-law.

At the time, I did not treat it like a serious matter, even though it could have put me in jail. But once I truly began seeking God and submitting to the sanctification process, I came to understand that it mattered greatly to Him. My walk with God seemed to be moving along just fine until, all at once, it felt like everything came to a halt. It was as though the Holy Spirit said, "If you want to keep moving forward, there are some things you must go back and repair."

He brought those moments of theft back to my mind with unmistakable clarity. If I was going to continue walking with God, then I had to make those wrongs right. I had to go to those people, confess what I had done, and ask them to forgive me. Forgiveness is one of the great keys to freedom. I believed God had forgiven me, and I believed I was saved, but I had not yet realized how important it was for my life on this earth to seek forgiveness from those I had wounded.

Now I watch for those moments along the road of life the way a driver watches for deer that might jump out in front of him at any moment.

Here's a slightly more memoir-style version too:

I decided that my relationship with God mattered more than my pride or my fear of consequences, so I chose to make things right. There I was, a grown man with a wife and children of my own, standing before my father-in-law and asking him to forgive me for stealing from him all those years earlier. I also wrote him a check to repay what I had taken. It was humbling, and it was hard. But that day I gained a new level of respect from my father-in-law, and in my spirit, I felt as though God was pleased.

Before long, it felt like I was back on the road, moving forward again with Jesus—until I passed the mall where there was a store from which I had stolen a cassette tape as a teenager. Oh no, not this again, I thought. I tried every way I could to justify it. It had only been petty theft. I had been young and stupid.

Surely it was not that big a deal. But it was a big deal to God, and if I wanted to keep moving forward, I knew I had to make that right as well.

I wrestled with it for months before I finally reached the point where I could not ignore it anymore. So I grabbed my checkbook and went to the store.

As I walked in, I secretly hoped the place had changed ownership over the years so I could be spared the embarrassment. But it had not. Nearly thirty years later, I found myself standing there, nervous and uncomfortable, asking if they were still the same owners from back in the 1980s. When they said yes, I knew there was no turning back.

So, I explained everything. I told them how I had stolen a cassette tape from their store as a teenager and how I had come back to make it right. The expression on their faces was unforgettable. By God's mercy, they were Christians, and they immediately understood what I was doing. They gladly forgave me and accepted my check for fifteen dollars to cover the loss.

And with that, I was back on the road of freedom once again.

These days, I watch for moments like that on the road of life the way a driver watches for deer along a dark highway, knowing they can appear without warning.

To many people, these things may seem petty or insignificant, but to God, sin is sin. Our understanding of forgiveness may determine whether we become heroes of faith or remain stagnant in our walk with Christ. God calls us to holiness because He is holy, and we will never walk in true holiness without learning to forgive.

We must forgive others, forgive ourselves, and, when necessary, seek forgiveness from those we have wronged. I believe some of our greatest spiritual growth happens in those moments when we must humble ourselves and ask another person to forgive us. Without humility, we cannot know God as deeply as He desires us to know Him.

Search the Scriptures and see what they say about humility and forgiveness. These are not optional qualities. They are essential for heroes of faith in the last days.

Chapter 10: Get Ready

In Acts 1 and 2, Jesus tells His disciples that they will be empowered by the Holy Spirit and will carry the gospel to Jerusalem, Judea, Samaria, and ultimately to the ends of the earth. Not long after, they experienced one of the most supernatural moments in Scripture as the Holy Spirit descended upon them, filling them with power and authority. Peter—the same man who had denied Jesus three times—rose to his feet and preached the message that set the gospel of Jesus Christ on a course that would change the world. In that moment, the church was born.

As the book of Acts unfolds, we are introduced to a man named Saul, who became one of the leading persecutors of the early church. He would later be gloriously converted and become Paul, but at that time he was feared for his hatred of Christians and his determination to have them arrested and imprisoned. Yet it was through that persecution that the gospel was driven outward into Judea and Samaria, just as Jesus had said it would be. What they did not yet understand was that trials, tribulation, and persecution would become part of the very engine God would use to spread the gospel.

The hatred directed at the church is nothing new, but the question is whether our response will resemble that of the early church. When our faith is attacked, will we respond in a way that spreads the gospel—whether intentionally or not—or will we shrink back, retreat behind the walls of our churches, and remain silent out of fear of consequences or fear of offending others?

If we truly believe we are living in the last days, then that conviction should be evident in both our words and our actions. We are stepping into a battle against evil that cannot be won by the watered-down Christianity so common in our time. Too often, faith has been treated like a product—something exciting when it feels new but easily exchanged for a more fashionable version when the novelty fades. Compromise has become so widespread that it is increasingly difficult to distinguish the church from the world.

This battle will only be won by those willing to walk in the kind of faith the early church possessed—a faith marked by dependence on the power of God rather than on technology, performance, or human charisma. Paul told the Corinthians that he did not come with eloquent speech or worldly wisdom, lest the cross of Christ be emptied of its power. He came in the demonstration of the Spirit and of power. That is the kind of faith required for the days ahead.

The battle lines are being drawn, and this conflict is far greater than politics, constitutional debates, or ideological movements. At its core, it is a battle between good and evil, truth and deception, righteousness and rebellion. And it is being fought in ways many of us never imagined we would see. I never thought I would live to see so many people openly embrace darkness and defend agendas that stand opposed to the truth of God.

So, if we truly believe we are living in the last days, what kind of people ought we to be? We ought to live holy and godly lives, making every effort to be found spotless, blameless, and at peace with Him. We ought to grow in the grace and knowledge of our Lord Jesus Christ. But those things do not happen accidentally. They are found only when we are centered in His will and committed to seeking truth—which means becoming devoted students of His Word. God has not changed. The church has.

At one point during His earthly ministry, the disciples noticed that Jesus had not eaten and urged Him to take some food. His response was profound: His food was to do the will of the Father and to finish His work (John 4:34 NIV). Imagine what would happen if we treated the Word of God and the will of God as though they were as essential to us as our next meal. If we carried the mind of Christ and understood that without truth we would die—which spiritually speaking, we will—what kind of impact might our lives have on the world around us?

We must become so hungry for the Word of God that it becomes our daily bread and our deepest craving. Our desire to accomplish His will must be so intense that we pursue Him with the urgency of a hunter searching for food to feed a starving family. A true warrior of faith understands that nothing in this world is more important than serving God and loving others—not work, not possessions, not comfort, and not even the priorities we often place above Him.

When the human body is deprived of proper nourishment, it becomes weak, unhealthy, and vulnerable to sickness. The same principle applies to the spirit. Without truth and regular communion with God, we become spiritually weak and lifeless. God did not create us merely to move from one job to another, trying to build a temporary life in a world that is destined to fade away. He created us to contend for what is eternal— for the things He has prepared for those who truly love Him.

The same idea can be seen in military service. A person may sign on the dotted line and raise their right hand, swearing to defend the Constitution of the United States, but that alone does not make them a true soldier. At that point, they are only a soldier by title. It is through the breaking down and rebuilding process of military training that a real soldier is formed. Through sweat, pain, discipline, and perseverance, they are transformed according to the standard required of them. Out of that process comes the mindset, confidence, and readiness of a true soldier.

A soldier is no longer expected to live as a civilian. He is called to a greater level of discipline and to a life that many are unwilling to live. In many ways, he lays down much of his own freedom so that others may continue to enjoy theirs.

As heroes of faith, we must take on that kind of mentality. Scripture calls us not to conform any longer to the pattern of this world, but to be transformed by the renewing of our minds. Only then will we be able to discern and embrace the will of God. We must let go of the casual attitude that says, "I'm going to make mistakes. God's not finished with me yet." While it is true that God is still at work in us, that truth must never be used to excuse sin.

Sin must be seen for what it is: failure. And failure must never become something we make peace with. The moment we accept it as just another part of life, we begin to justify it. Instead, we must understand that sin is the line between walking in the Spirit and living in the flesh. It separates us from God and leads toward death. Sin is an enemy, and it must be treated as one. It drains us of the spiritual power God intends for us to walk in daily. We cannot expect great spiritual victories while continuing to indulge the flesh and tolerate ongoing sin. We must be transformed rather than conformed if the Spirit of God is to move freely and powerfully in our lives.

And yet, when we do stumble, we are not without hope. We can be grateful that when we confess our sins, He is faithful and just to forgive us and to cleanse us from all unrighteousness.

I believe God is raising up new heroes of faith for these last days—men and women who have been humbled by their weaknesses, failures, and mistakes. These are people willing to do whatever pleases God and whatever is necessary to fight the good fight. They are warriors who are dying to the flesh daily instead of conforming to it or compromising with it. They are soldiers who will not be overtaken by the distractions of this age or become more devoted to a denomination than to Christ the King. God is raising up an army that believes in the true power of the Holy Spirit as revealed in Scripture, not in a shallow substitute or a cheap imitation.

If you are reading this and something in you is stirring to become a true hero of faith, know this: you are not alone. I want that too. I fight for it every day. At times, I catch glimpses of that kind of faith, but only in flashes. I know it is there, yet it often feels just beyond my reach because, in this season, my defeats against the flesh seem to outnumber my victories.

So, when will I attain the kind of faith required to be a spiritual hero? It will happen when I become a slave to righteousness and fully understand that this kind of life cannot be achieved through my own effort or accomplishments, but only through the sanctifying power of the blood of Christ. Becoming a Christian is free, but becoming a hero of faith requires a life of surrender, discipline, and obedience. We can choose to settle for a softened, human-centered version of Christianity, or we can rise above it and become biblically grounded heroes of faith.

All throughout Scripture, God set people apart for His purposes. Many of them were unlikely choices by human standards, but God has never chosen His soldiers according to the wisdom of man. He sees in us what we cannot yet see in ourselves. Through His Spirit, He can draw out the gifts, strength, and calling He placed within us from the very beginning. You may look in the mirror and see failure, but God may be looking at a chosen warrior.

The question is not, "Is God real?" The deeper question is, "Am I?" Will I choose to become that chosen warrior, rise above the flesh, and follow God into battle? Or will I conform to a commercialized, diluted form of faith? A true hero of faith must come to terms with the fact that trials, tribulations, and suffering will often come at a level many others will never know, simply because he has chosen to walk the road Christ set before him. He will be different, and the world will treat him accordingly.

The truth spoken by a hero of faith will not only convict the sinner, but it will also wound the hearts of many who claim the name of Christ while clinging to false teachings and man-made ideas. And above all, a true hero of faith never takes credit for what God alone has done. His own name fades into the background, while the name of Abba Father is lifted high.

As I wrote this book, I resisted the urge to start listing the people who have inspired us, helped us, and walked beside us through so many seasons. I could have easily devoted an entire chapter to the friends and family who have supported us every step of the way. But it became deeply important to me that the only name receiving glory in these pages be the name of Jesus.

I am grateful beyond words for our friends and family, but this book was written to declare that Jesus is the way, the truth, and the life, and that through the sanctifying power of His blood, He can take the world's greatest failures and turn them into heroes. So do not give up. Do not quit simply because life does not appear to be going the way you hoped, because it may be unfolding exactly as God intended. If you see yourself as a nothing or a nobody, know this: God wants you. And He is able to transform you into a warrior unlike anything you ever imagined.

Not everyone who reads this book will agree with it. I am sure some will question it, and others may even take offense at what I have written. But I have simply shared what God placed on my heart, along with my own experiences, in the hope that it might help someone else see how deeply personal He desires to be with us. We can never sin ourselves beyond His reach, and we are never too far gone for Him to redeem and use. We must come to know Him for ourselves and seek truth as if our very lives depend on it. There may be few who choose to become heroes of faith, but as Jeremiah 5 reminds us, sometimes only one is needed.

Epilogue

As I come to the end of this book, I find myself thinking again about courage.

Not the kind of courage the world usually celebrates. Not the kind built on image, applause, or the need to win an argument. I mean the quieter kind. The kind that is willing to stand when standing is costly. The kind that keeps speaking when silence would be easier. The kind that refuses to bow simply because pressure has increased.

In every generation, there are people who remind us what that kind of courage looks like.

Charlie Kirk is one example that comes to mind. Whatever views people may hold about him, he was clearly willing to stand in the public eye and speak with conviction in a time when many would rather avoid the cost of doing so. In a world where fear, compromise, and silence often seem easier, that kind of boldness stands out.

I do not say that to make this about politics. That is not the point. The point is that courage still matters.

Boldness still matters.

And a willingness to stand for what one believes still matters.

But as this book has tried to show, courage by itself is not enough. True courage must be rooted in something deeper than personality or passion. It must be anchored in truth. It must be shaped by humility. It must be surrendered to God. Otherwise, even boldness can become just another expression of self.

A last days hero is not simply someone who knows how to speak loudly. A last days hero is someone who knows how to stand faithfully.

That kind of person may never be famous.

They may never have a microphone, a platform, or a crowd. But heaven sees them.

They are the ones who remain true when compromise would be easier. They are the ones who keep believing when the world grows darker.

They are the ones who keep loving, keep praying, keep obeying, and keep standing when others grow tired.

That is the kind of courage I hope for. Not just in public figures.

Not just in people we admire from a distance. But in us.

In me. In you.

In the people of God.

Because in the days ahead, the question will not be whether we can recognize courage in someone else. The question will be whether we are willing to live it ourselves.

And that, perhaps, is where the search for the last days hero truly ends.

Not in admiration. But in surrender.

Not in pointing to someone else.

But in asking God to make us faithful.

Last Days Heroes Bible Study Guide

How to Use This Study Guide

This guide is designed to accompany Last Days Heroes as either a personal devotional study or a small-group Bible study.

- Each session includes:
- a main theme
- suggested reading from the book
- key Scriptures
- A session summary
- Discussions
- personal reflection
- Prayer Focus
- An action step for the week

You can use one session per week or move at whatever pace fits your group.

Suggested Group Format

- Opening prayer
- Review of previous week's action step
- Read key Scripture passages
- Discuss chapter theme and questions
- Quiet personal reflection

- Share prayer requests
- Closing prayer
- Commit to the weekly action step

Session 1:
The Call of the Last Days Hero

Based on: Introduction

Main focus: What kind of person is God looking for in the last days?

Key Scriptures

2 Peter 3:10–14

Matthew 24:3–14

Romans 13:11–14

Session Summary

The last days are not meant to produce panic in the people of God, but preparation. Scripture calls believers to wake up, live with urgency, and pursue holiness in light of Christ's return. The question is not merely whether we believe we are in the last days, but whether we are living like it. God is looking for people who are awake, truthful, faithful, and ready.

Discussion Questions

When you hear the phrase "the last days," what emotions or thoughts come to mind first?

Why do you think some believers become more fascinated with prophecy than with personal holiness?

According to 2 Peter 3, how should the coming of the Lord affect the way we live now?

What does spiritual readiness look like in everyday life?

What is one area of your life where you need to become more spiritually alert?

Personal Reflection

Read Romans 13:11–14 slowly. Ask yourself: Am I spiritually awake, or have I become passive? Where have I grown casual in my walk with God?

Prayer Focus

Ask God to awaken your heart, deepen your hunger for holiness, and make you spiritually ready for the days ahead.

Action Step for the Week

Choose one habit that will help you live more intentionally this week, such as setting aside daily prayer time, reading Scripture first each morning, or removing one distraction that dulls your spiritual focus.

Session 2: What Makes a Hero?

Based on: Chapter 1

Main focus: Understanding true heroism through sacrifice, courage, and faith

Key Scriptures

John 15:13

Hebrews 11:1–6

Psalm 78:4–7

Session Summary

The world often defines heroism by fame, power, or public recognition. But many of the people who shape our lives most deeply are known for sacrifice, faithfulness, and courage. This session explores how God's view of a hero is often very different from the world's, and how personal stories of courage can point us toward deeper spiritual truth.

Discussion Questions

Who has been a hero in your life, and why?

What is the difference between worldly heroism and biblical faithfulness?

Why is sacrifice such an important part of true heroism?

How can ordinary people become examples of courage and faith to others?

In what ways does Hebrews 11 expand or challenge your definition of a hero?

Personal Reflection

Think about one person whose faith or courage shaped your life. What qualities in them most reflected Christ?

Prayer Focus

Thank God for the people who have modeled courage, sacrifice, and faith in your life. Ask Him to make your life a source of strength to others.

Action Step for the Week

Encourage one person who has quietly been a hero in your life. Send a note, make a call, or tell them specifically how they have impacted you.

Session 3:
The One God Could Not Find

Based on: Chapter 2

Main focus: Standing in the gap when truth is scarce

Key Scriptures

Jeremiah 5:1

Ezekiel 22:30

Jonah 3:1–10

Session Summary

In Jeremiah 5, God was looking for one person who dealt honestly and sought the truth. The tragedy was not only the sin of the people, but the absence of someone willing to stand in the gap. This session challenges us to consider whether we are willing to be people of truth, righteousness, and mercy in a culture that resists all three.

Discussion Questions

What stands out to you most about Jeremiah 5:1?

Why do you think truth and righteousness were so hard to find in that moment?

What does it mean to "stand in the gap" for others?

How does Jonah's attitude toward Nineveh challenge our own hearts?

Are there people or places you are more tempted to judge than to intercede for?

Personal Reflection

Ask yourself whether you are more likely to pray for mercy or to wish for judgment when you see wickedness around you.

Prayer Focus

Ask God to make you a truthful, righteous, and merciful person who can stand in the gap for others.

Action Step for the Week

Spend time praying for one person, city, or situation you have previously felt cynical or angry about. Pray for

repentance, mercy, and God's intervention.

Session 4:
Marks of a Hero of Faith

Based on: Chapter 3

Main focus: Holiness, obedience, truth, and action

Key Scriptures

Colossians 3:1–17

James 2:14–18

John 14:15

Session Summary

A hero of faith does not simply believe the right things. A hero of faith lives them. This session looks at how truth, obedience, holiness, and action all work together in the life of a real disciple. Faith that never changes how we live is incomplete.

Discussion Questions

Why is it possible to claim faith without really walking in it?

What does Colossians 3 reveal about what should be put off and what should be put on?

How do obedience and love for Christ connect according to John 14:15?

What does James mean when he says faith without works is dead?

What is one area where your faith needs to move from intention to action?

Personal Reflection

Read Colossians 3 and write down one attitude or habit you need to put away, and one Christlike quality you need to pursue.

Prayer Focus

Ask God to make your faith active, obedient, and visible in the way you live.

Action Step for the Week

Choose one practical act of obedience this week that reflects your faith, such as serving someone, making something right, or stepping away from a compromise you have tolerated.

Session 5:
Seeing the Unseen Battle

Based on: Chapters 4–5

Main focus: Spiritual warfare, discernment, and guarding open doors

Key Scriptures

Ephesians 6:10–18

1 Peter 5:8–9

2 Corinthians 10:3–5

Session Summary

The Christian life includes real spiritual conflict. Believers are called to be sober, alert, and discerning without becoming fearful or obsessive. This session focuses on the reality of the unseen battle, the importance of guarding what we allow into our lives, and the necessity of standing in Christ's authority rather than our own strength.

Discussion Questions

Why do many Christians either ignore spiritual warfare or become unbalanced about it?

What does Ephesians 6 teach us about how to stand against the enemy?

What kinds of "open doors" might weaken a believer spiritually?

Why is discernment different from fear?

How can we stay focused on Christ instead of becoming fascinated with darkness?

Personal Reflection

Take inventory of what influences your home, life, entertainment choices, and habits. Is there anything you need to remove, renounce, or bring under the lordship of Christ?

Prayer Focus

Ask God for discernment, spiritual protection, and the strength to stand firm in Christ.

Action Step for the Week

Identify one area of spiritual compromise or unhealthy influence in your life and take a concrete step to shut that door.

Session 6: Hearing and Obeying God's Voice

Based on: Chapter 6

Main focus: Learning to recognize God's leading

Key Scriptures

John 10:27

Romans 8:14

Isaiah 30:21

Session Summary

God still leads His people. He speaks primarily through His Word, but He also impresses things on the heart by His Spirit and directs His people in practical ways. The issue is not only whether we believe God speaks, but whether we are willing to listen and obey when He does.

Discussion Questions

What are healthy, biblical ways God leads His people?

Why is it important to test impressions by Scripture?

How does obedience strengthen our sensitivity to God's voice?

Have you ever sensed God leading you to do something simple but meaningful?

What usually keeps people from obeying God's prompting?

Personal Reflection

Think about a time you sensed God's leading. Did you obey? What did you learn from the outcome?

Prayer Focus

Ask God to make you sensitive to His voice, anchored in His Word, and quick to obey.

Action Step for the Week

Ask the Lord each morning to lead you that day. Pay attention to one specific prompting that aligns with Scripture and obey it.

Session 7:
Becoming a Link to Hope

Based on: Chapter 7

Main focus: Calling, suffering, and connecting people to Christ

Key Scriptures

2 Corinthians 1:3–7

Romans 8:28

Matthew 5:14–16

Session Summary

God often uses our deepest pain to prepare us to minister to others. What He comforts in us can become something He pours through us. This session explores how calling is not about self-promotion, but about becoming a living connection between hurting people and the hope found in Christ.

Discussion Questions

How can suffering prepare a person for ministry?

What does it mean to be a "link to hope" for someone else?

Why is calling different from ambition?

How can pain become part of someone's testimony without becoming their identity?

Where might God be asking you to offer hope from a place where you have also known pain?

Personal Reflection

What trial or painful season has God used to deepen your compassion or shape your calling?

Prayer Focus

Ask God to redeem your pain and use your story to bring hope to others.

Action Step for the Week

Encourage one hurting person this week with a note, conversation, prayer, or act of kindness rooted in

Christ's hope.

Session 8:
The Fall and the Mercy of God

Based on: Chapter 8

Main focus: Failure, repentance, and restoration

Key Scriptures

Psalm 51

Luke 15:11–24

1 John 1:9

Session Summary

Growing up around faith is not the same as truly surrendering to God. This session examines the danger of outward religion without inward transformation, and the mercy of God toward those who fall deeply but genuinely return to Him. The goal is not to glorify failure, but to magnify redemption.

Discussion Questions

Why is borrowed faith not enough to sustain a person?

What is the difference between guilt and true repentance?

What do Psalm 51 and Luke 15 reveal about God's heart toward the repentant?

Why do people sometimes hide behind outward religion instead of real surrender?

How does God's mercy give hope to those who feel they have fallen too far?

Personal Reflection

Bring before God any area where you need honest repentance, not just regret. Ask Him to search your heart and restore what has been damaged.

Prayer Focus

Thank God for His mercy and ask Him to produce real repentance, healing, and restoration.

Action Step for the Week

Read Psalm 51 aloud as a personal prayer. Write down one area where you need to invite God's cleansing and renewal.

Session 9: Fighting the Real War

Based on: Chapter 9

Main focus: The spiritual battle of the age and the call to holiness

Key Scriptures

Romans 12:1–2

2 Corinthians 4:3–4

1 Thessalonians 4:3–8

Session Summary

The deepest war of our time is spiritual. It cannot be won through outrage, image, or human strength. It must be fought through repentance, holiness, truth, and obedience. This session calls believers to reject compromise and live as real disciples in a darkening world.

Discussion Questions

In what ways is the real battle of our time spiritual rather than merely cultural or political?

Why does compromise weaken a believer's witness and discernment?

What does it mean to offer your body as a living sacrifice?

Why is repentance still essential in the life of a believer?

What areas of compromise are most dangerous to Christians today?

Personal Reflection

Ask God to reveal any compromise in your life that is weakening your walk, your witness, or your spiritual strength.

Prayer Focus

Pray for holiness, repentance, and courage to live distinctly for Christ in a compromised culture.

Action Step for the Week

Choose one area where you need to draw a clearer line of obedience, and act on it this week.

Session 10:
Get Ready

Based on: Chapter 10

Main focus: Readiness, Spirit-filled obedience, and the cost of discipleship

Key Scriptures

Acts 1:8

Acts 8:26–40

Acts 9:10–19

Matthew 25:1–13

Session Summary

The early church was marked by power, surrender, courage, and obedience. As pressure increased, the gospel still moved forward. This final session calls believers to get ready—to live with spiritual urgency, to obey when God says go, and to become the kind of disciples who are prepared for whatever He asks.

Discussion Questions

What qualities made the early church spiritually strong?

Why is readiness such a major theme in Scripture?

What does it look like to be ready for God's assignment in ordinary life?

Where do comfort and convenience most interfere with obedience?

After this study, what is one clear way God is calling you to respond?

Personal Reflection

Ask yourself whether your current life reflects readiness, complacency, or delay. What would it look like to

live prepared for God's next instruction?

Prayer Focus

Ask God to make you ready—filled with His Spirit, grounded in His Word, courageous in obedience, and faithful to the end.

Action Step for the Week

Write down one specific step of obedience God is asking of you right now and commit to take it.

Closing Encouragement

The goal of this study is not merely to gain information, but to become the kind of people God can use. A hero of faith is not someone perfect, famous, or naturally strong. A hero of faith is someone surrendered, obedient, truthful, and willing to let God work through an ordinary life for eternal purposes.

May God use this study to deepen your faith, sharpen your discernment, strengthen your obedience, and prepare you to stand in the days ahead.